LIBRARY TRAINING GUIDES

Mentoring

Biddy Fisher

Library Association Publishing

© Library Association Publishing Ltd 1994

Published by
Library Association Publishing Ltd
7 Ridgmount Street
London WC1E 7AE

First published 1994

British Library Cataloguing in Publication Data. A catalogue record for this book is available from the British Library.

ISBN 1-85604-105-0

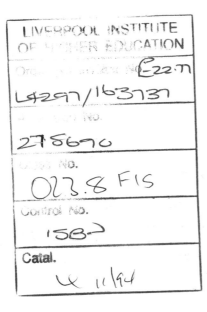
Typeset in 11/12pt Palermo from author's disk by Library Association Publishing Ltd
Printed and made in Great Britain by Amber (Printwork) Ltd, Harpenden, Herts.

Introduction by the Series Editor

This new series of Library Training Guides (LTGs for short) aims to fill the gap left by the demise of the old Training Guidelines published in the 1980s in the wake of the Library Association's work on staff training. The new LTGs develop the original concept of concisely written summaries of the best principles and practice in specific areas of training by experts in the field which give library and information workers a good-quality guide to best practice. Like the original guidelines, the LTGs also include appropriate examples from a variety of library systems as well as further reading and useful contacts.

Though each guide stands in its own right, LTGs form a coherent whole. Acquisition of all LTGs as they are published will result in a comprehensive manual of training and staff development in library and information work.

The guides are aimed at practising librarians and library training officers. They are intended to be comprehensive without being over-detailed; they should give both the novice and the experienced librarian/training officer an overview of what should/could be done in a given situation and in relation to a particular skill/group of library staff/type of library.

David Baker

LIBRARY TRAINING GUIDES

Series Editor: David Baker
Editorial Assistant: Joan Welsby

Introduction by the Series Editor

This new series of Library Training Guides (LTGs for short) aims to fill the gap left by the demise of the old Training Guidelines published in the 1980s in the wake of the Library Association's work on staff training. The new LTGs develop the original concept of concisely written summaries of the best principles and practice in specific areas of training by experts in the field which give library and information workers a good-quality guide to best practice. Like the original guidelines, the LTGs also include appropriate examples from a variety of library systems as well as further reading and useful contacts.

Though each guide stands in its own right, LTGs form a coherent whole. Acquisition of all LTGs as they are published will result in a comprehensive manual of training and staff development in library and information work.

The guides are aimed at practising librarians and library training officers. They are intended to be comprehensive without being over-detailed; they should give both the novice and the experienced librarian/training officer an overview of what should/could be done in a given situation and in relation to a particular skill/group of library staff/type of library.

David Baker

Contents

Preface

Structure of this guide

This guide has been designed to assist those wishing to review mentoring for its application to a particular workplace. Chapters 2 and 3 deal with the main roles of those engaged in a mentoring system. Chapter 4 describes the skills and characteristics which mentors should develop. Chapter 5 describes models of formal mentoring systems and offers examples drawn from a variety of organizations and indicates the organizational requirements for introducing mentoring as well as the process. Other forms of mentoring are illustrated in Chapter 6 and Chapter 7 summarizes the main themes of the guide.

Mention is made of mentoring systems in a range of organizations but few exist in library and information services in the United Kingdom. Appendix A is a selective bibliography of the available literature of mentoring in the UK and United States of America. Sample training programmes from organizations are provided in Appendix C.

Sources of information

As a starting point the invaluable Bath Information Data Services (BIDS) was accessed. This provides a database of references and citations in the social sciences and from it a range of journal references was obtained. It should be noted that the subject is inter-disciplinary and ranges between social, management and psychological subject areas, therefore databases for management as well as librarianship were also explored.

Professional organizations such as The Institute of Management, The Institute of Manpower Studies and Women in Technology (WIT) have been willing to share their approach to the subject. Other organizations, notably the BBC and ICL, generously provided examples of documents used by their training and development departments. The addresses of several organizations prepared to offer advice on mentoring appear in Appendix B.

Management consultants and training organizations have been amongst the most helpful of advisers and have provided valuable examples of their training guides. Jenny Sweeney of The Industrial Society, Joanna Howard of Roffey Park Management Institute, Dr Gill Burrington (The Burrington Partnership), Christine Williams, Membership Development Manager of the Institute of Personnel Management, and especially David Clutterbuck of the European Mentoring Centre and Steve Carter of the Institute of Management, all provided information and documentation which supported the production of the guide.

Individuals have provided evidence which substantiates the claims in the literature which are frequently made, despite the lack of research in the area. Despite many leads it was not possible to trace one library organization which used a formal mentoring scheme, or any other institution containing a library system which practised mentoring on any substantial scale.

A personal note from the author

When starting the background work for this training guide I was struck by the need for mentors to be absolute paragons. Their behaviour had to be exemplary, their integrity beyond question, and their experience complete. Surely no one could achieve this and still be living? Having read Gill Burrington's[1] collection of the real experiences of women who had reached management positions I came to realize that there are many people who influence all our careers. It was the term mentor that was new, not the experience. The people who are identified as mentors in *Equally good* are all ordinary people. Their experiences are not unique, but they all have the ability and generosity of spirit to want to share this with other, less experienced people and an altruistic belief that this may provide a good foundation for their protégés.

The other conclusion which I reached was that, like many management techniques, mentoring was a particular combination of a range of skills which are used in other contexts. The transferability of skills is a much underrated concept and is frequently misunderstood. Many of the readings deal with the systems of mentoring; they refer to the specific skills required but do not engage with the **processes** of mentoring and the way in which it is necessary to combine skills and techniques into these processes which perpetuate the systems.

What has been difficult is the selection of acceptable terms which describe adequately the roles within mentoring. Anyone with a passing knowledge of the French language will soon realize that I have used the male form of protégé to indicate both males and females. I would have preferred to find a non-gender-specific word, but the language does not provide for this without detracting from the import of the term. Therefore I can only offer apologies to those who find this unacceptable.

The Library Training Guides (LTGs for short) have a particular aim to create a practical guide to particular areas. It is hoped that the approach which has been adopted in this guide supports the aim of the series for the variety of readers who pick this remarkable topic.

I am grateful to all the organizations mentioned here, and to the many others who have helped in the preparation of this guide.

Reference

1   Burrington, G., *Equally good*, London, Association of Assistant Librarians, 1993.

Introduction

At least two of the Library Training Guides (LTGs) contain references to mentoring: as a specific practice to enhance the process of assimilation and induction into a new working environment,[1] and as a career planning tactic which women can apply to their career development plan as discussed by Beryl Morris.[2]

1.1 Brief history of mentoring

Mentoring is not a new concept. The first mention of it and the titular hero of this book was an ancient Greek, chosen by Odysseus (Ulysses) to look after his son, the young Telemachus, while away on his epic voyage of discovery. There was more to the instruction than just keeping a paternal eye on the young man, and grooming Telemachus for his eventual position as head of state was a priority. This was achieved by advising, encouraging and teaching, by providing counselling and a role model, and by passing on the experience which the older man possessed to the younger.

It is also interesting to note that Greek mythology also allows for Mentor to be a woman and take the form appropriate to the situation via the goddess, Athene.

Whichever tale is chosen the result is an accepted and logical way of the old assisting the young to reach their goals and become the next generation of wise men and women. There are historical figures who at first would seem to exhibit the characteristics of mentoring but for one reason or another have failed. In the literary world there are exploitative examples such as Willy and Colette, or in literature the George du Maurier story of Svengali and Trilby, both of which illustrate the need for altruism on the part of the mentor if a true mentoring relationship is to be established. In contemporary life, the relationship between Bobby Charlton and the late Sir Matt Busby is an example of the mentor relationship at its best.

There has been sufficient interest in the historical study of mentoring to justify an article by Head and Gray[3] devoted to the identification of mentors throughout history and readers will have their own ideas about the particular relationships between the famous and the gifted who have passed on the benefits of experience in various disciplines.

1.2 Contemporary mentoring

American businesses were swift to understand the benefits for all if mentoring was promoted and encouraged. British business, cautious or even sceptical of the American management education, was slow to develop formal mentoring. However, it did rely for a large part on the 'old boy' network, not dissimilar to informal mentoring. It is now recognized that it needs more than serendipity or a gender-oriented network to ensure that employees are given the best opportunities for self and career development. Introducing mentoring means formalizing a system of pairing experienced employees with those who have particular needs in their work environment. In this way it can have a significant effect on morale, motivation and quality of working life within an organization.

While recognized as an effective form of professional training and development, there is no widely accepted format for a mentoring system which can be adapted or offered as a model of best practice. Part of the problem lies in the commonly held view that mentoring is a personal relationship which two people develop, in order to meet the development requirements of the mentored or protégé, with assistance from the mentor. This perception needs to be broadened, for it is possible for an organization to introduce mentoring as part of a planned programme of development, for new employees and existing staff. It is also useful when an organization is undergoing change.

1.3 The mentoring arrangement

Mentoring implies a certain relationship between individuals. Each mentoring arrangement will be unique, and its particular nature will be established according to the very personalities of the two individuals concerned. Mentoring is a learning process. It is part of the system in which we engage, when life poses questions for which we are not prepared. Alan Mumford,[4] in a work commissioned by the Manpower Services Commission in 1987, investigated the management development processes followed by 144 directors in 41 British businesses in their managerial careers. 'Incidental learning', as he named it, arose from dealing with situations. The additional help which trusted mentors can offer is a valuable asset in a learning process. They will not judge or instruct, they will facilitate or interpret and empower the protégé to arrive at his/her own decision.

Mentoring describes a particular system of communication using a specific set of skills and body of knowledge, tailor-made for a particular arrangement between a mentor and a protégé. Thus it is a term which embodies ambiguity, for it refers to both a system and a specific relationship between two people. An organization can introduce and support a mentoring system. Equally an individual may choose a mentor without reference to an employer. No existing mentoring arrangement precludes the start of another, and individuals may choose to develop more than one mentoring arrangement with particular individuals for specific needs. A mentoring arrangement should be flexible and organic. It serves a particular need which, with time, may diminish or disappear.

Individuals can agree to a mentoring arrangement within, or quite separate from, an organization-specific scheme for human resource management. If established by an organization it is usually chosen to assist in the motivation and development of new and existing employees. This is a formal mentoring scheme and will have certain rules attached to it although there will be room for considerable interpretation by the individuals concerned. It is not possible to discuss formal mentoring without acknowledging the existence of informal mentoring, which for many will be the more common practice.

1.4 The practice of mentoring

The freedom with which a protégé can choose a mentor is a powerful factor for success in informal mentoring, as Michael Zey[5] concludes. This should not in any way negate the usefulness of the process for organizations. However, there are factors relating to the nature of the organization which must be achieved if mentoring is to be successful. An organization wishing to introduce mentoring must address two main areas. Firstly, the establishment of a learning culture with a high degree of priority given to training and development for employees. Secondly an emphasis on the achievement of high quality in terms of service and 'customer care' which should permeate the whole organization, not just those with the particular responsibility for meeting the external users of the service.

The practice of mentoring, however established, will exhibit common characteristics, including the special skills required of the mentor in a number of key roles, and the nature of the arrangement which is essentially voluntary. Organizational mentoring will, in addition, require more formal documentation and training for those who will act as mentors, together with preparation for both parties.

It is essential to recognize the problems and pitfalls which may occur in any mentoring arrangement. Some may be foreseen and therefore avoided; others will require the application of problem-solving techniques in order to avoid destructive situations developing. Like any other technique used in human resource development, mentoring has a particular application which may prove unsuitable for some people. In establishing mentoring as part of a human resource development system, care must be taken to ensure that each person knows the limits or boundaries of the relationship. In formal systems of mentoring it is as important to indicate that there is a way out as it is to encourage the development of the relationship in the first place.

References

1 Parry, J., *Induction*, London, Library Association Publishing Limited, 1993.
2 Morris, B., *Training and development for women*, London, Library Association Publishing Limited, 1993.
3 Head, F. and Gray, M. M., 'The legacy of Mentor: insights into western history, literature and the media', *International journal of mentoring*, **2** (2), 1988, 26–33.
4 Mumford, A., *Developing directors: the learning process*, London, Manpower Services Commission, 1987.
5 Zey, M., 'Mentoring programmes: making the right moves', *Personnel journal*, **64** (2), 1985, 53–7.

2 The mentor

What is a mentor?

There is no position of 'mentor'. It cannot be applied for, and there is no competition to attain it. Many definitions of 'mentor' exist; some are qualified in some way, as for example major and minor mentors described by Darling,[1] life or career mentors mentioned by Dodgson[2] and primary or secondary mentors referred to by Phillips-Jones.[3]

The classical definition includes reference to the personal and the professional aspects of the mentor/protégé relationship but there are no exclusions, for each relationship will create its own dynamic, and will develop its own criteria for the boundaries of its existence. Most writers on this topic will readily accede to the idea that while an individual may have many partial mentors who work with them on certain aspects of their life, there can only be one primary mentor. Likewise it is understood that life mentors can be career mentors, but rarely can career mentors be life mentors.

Darling[1] offers a rule of thumb which can be applied by those wishing to draw a distinction between the major and minor, secondary or primary, which is that an **attraction** will exist between the mentor and protégé, that the mentor will take **action** on behalf of the protégé and that in terms of support and encouragement, the protégé will be **affected** by the mentor in a positive way. If any of these three attributes are missing from the relationship, then it can be classified as a secondary, minor or partial mentoring relationship.

The primary mentoring role can rarely be taken by someone who is not in a hierarchical position above that of the protégé within the same organization. If they are in a lower position than the protégé, the formality of a mentoring scheme would place this relationship within the definitions of partial or secondary mentoring.

Professions such as librarianship will have produced many people whose career has been influenced by the wisdom or advice offered to them while in the early stages of their career. Burrington[4] identified four individuals who established reputations for mentoring even though, at that time, there was no verb to describe the process.

2.2 Characteristics of a mentor

A precise definition is difficult to provide but the common characteristics of a mentor include:

- intelligence and integrity
- ability
- professional attitude
- high personal standards
- enthusiasm

- willingness to share accumulated knowledge

Mentors must be flexible and willing to accept any decision made by the protégé, whatever the consequences. Thus mentors must not judge or instruct, as this would be counter-productive to their role. By pre-empting the range of options which lie in front of anyone, a mentor will provide the guidance towards making a right decision. Ultimately though, they have no responsibility for the decision made by the protégé. Their role is to indicate the actual or potential effects of making a particular decision, and to offer a range of options from which the protégé makes a choice, and thereby takes responsibility for his/her own actions.

2.3 Roles for mentors

Among the roles of a mentor the following are common:

- facilitator
- counsellor
- advisor
- guide
- co-ordinator
- assessor
- role model
- opener of doors
- confidant
- communicator
- bridge
- link
- partner
- friend

A mentor plays an important role in the development of a protégé. In systems implemented within organizations, mentors are established to act as a guide and a supporting figure in the workplace. They can provide career counselling, act as role models, and offer introductions and contacts in order to pave the way to success of the person they mentor.

Carter[5] identifies the career functions and psychosocial functions of mentors. Formal mentoring schemes will focus on the former, while the latter are more dependent on areas beyond the control of an organization. In many cases, the relationship develops so that the interpersonal aspects provide 'confirmation of self-worth and facilitative support'.[5]

2.4 What is the purpose of the mentor?

To allow new people to observe departmental activities, divisional functions and goals, in addition to the polices and procedures of the organization through consultation with the experienced professional.[6]

Mentors assist the integration of new personnel into an organization, and do so by introducing them to other people within the organization.

Mentors can provide a bridge between the aims and objectives of an organization and its newest employees. By knowing the former, they can ensure that the latter obtain a sense of what is expected of them, as well as indicating how they can contribute effectively.

2.5 What are the mentors expected to do?

1 Mentors provide advice and feedback on performance within an organization's scheme. This will be specifically relevant to the needs of the organization.
2 It is expected that a mentor will offer constructive criticism.
3 Mentors listen: this is the critical exercise and the skill of effective listening is examined in section 4.2.2.
4 Mentors have to be able to identify the situations described by their protégés.
5 Mentors have to confront a range of behaviours from their protégés and deal with them effectively.
6 Mentors have to share their knowledge and experience, and offer information as required. In encouraging protégés to examine options for action, the mentor has to be able to pass on the responsibility for the outcome of any decision.

All these can be viewed as learning processes for the protégé. Good mentoring will encourage this good practice – to be replicated by the protégé, not just in work situations but through life in general.

2.6 Mentors may not . . .

There are instances of behaviour which mentors should not exhibit. For whatever good motives, mentors should not allow their feedback to become criticism which is destructive.

Their advice must be offered in such a way that it can be taken on as the protégé's own ideas. They may suggest a way out, but not provide the means of escape, or deal with the situation for the protégé.

The differences between good and bad mentors is illustrated by Carter[5] and reproduced in the table.

Good mentors	Bad mentors
1 Permissive not authoritarian Well informed Analytical	Too directive Opinionated Dogmatic Negative
2 Commitment to training Commitment to development	Not aware of value of staff training No experience or interest in staff
3 Good communicator Good open questioner Good listener	Poor communicator Uses closed questions Poor listener
4 Good knowledge of organization	Knowledge limited to department/section
5 Can apply theory to practice	Not really well educated No real understanding of management theory
6 Well organized	Disorganized Credibility in question

| 7 Knowledge of value of action learning | Lacks clarity Insensitive to process |
| 8 Good time manager: time devoted to role of mentor | Poor manager: always insufficient time for mentor role |

2.7 Can my line manager be my mentor?

This is possible, and Ferriero's 1982 survey[7] indicated that most mentors were the immediate supervisor. However, the evidence from this survey deals primarily with informal mentoring. In formal schemes, it is more likely that a mentor will not be involved in immediate line management responsibilities. The mentor may, however, advise the protégé's line manager. Thus the boundaries of responsibility may merge at times. (See section 5.2.3.)

2.8 Similarities or differences between mentor and protégé?

A mentor within an organization's system should have had a similar career path, be within a similar profession, or be seen as a senior whose position matches the aspirations of the protégé. It is important that the mentor understands the work of the protégé and what is needed by and of both of them, in order to achieve the agreed outcomes of the relationship.

2.9 Is there a future for mentors?

The study by Ferriero[7] in 1982 included a survey of the 111 directors of American research libraries. The results showed an involvement in mentoring by 77% of respondents. A recent survey by The Industrial Society, showed that 40% of the organizations surveyed had a formal programme of mentoring, compared with 30% in the previous survey carried out in 1989. 19% of other firms state they are actively seeking to implement a formal scheme, compared with 9% in 1989. The mentor has taken over from the line manager or 'coach' in the development process.

Other organizations are now seeking to implement mentoring schemes, including The Institute of Personnel Management for new IPM students and members, while The Library Association has begun the process by introducing the Framework for Professional Development. This is currently 'mentorless', but wise librarians using the profile will quickly establish the need for such a person as they sustain the impetus for the framework over the years.

2.10 Are there benefits for the mentor?

There is a certain personal satisfaction which cannot be quantified in being a mentor to a younger person. The characteristics and skills which mentors have are invaluable, but it is even more satisfying to have them utilized in a very personal situation.

By clarifying and articulating thoughts and ideas for another, a mentor gains experience in strategic thinking in a considerable variety of situations beyond their own immediate experience. The analytical and objective thinking required of a mentor develops a skill which many would wish to achieve. It is different from the strategic thinking of the manager or supervisor, who will have a different set of priorities to consider, not least of which will be the responsibility for other members of the department or division.

The one-to-one nature of mentoring allows for quality time with another person. This inevitably leads to greater understanding of oneself, one's motives and effectively a process of re-evaluation of a personal philosophy. Many mentors find that they gain greater understanding of human nature and of the organization in which they work, by having to advise and interpret issues with another.

There are always benefits to helping others, and the 'feel-good' factor should not be ignored. There is considerable confidence to be gained in undertaking the mentoring role, as skills are developed and confirmed.

For librarians, the need to seek out information is second nature, and having to provide this role for a protégé means adding to one's own knowledge. The more challenging aspect of mentoring is having to respond to a new set of ideas and to assimilate a different position on certain issues. It is this role which requires an open mind and unbiased opinions.

2.11 Summary

In summary, a mentoring relationship must attempt to be positive at all times, and must not involve any 'game playing'. The honesty required by a mentor may be difficult to maintain in the face of a decision made by the protégé which fails to reach the required outcome. This must be used by the mentor as a subsequent learning experience for the protégé, not as a lesson in failure.

2.12 Mentor case study

During the course of the research for this guide, some individuals provided valuable insight into their own experiences of mentoring. An interview with Sheila Corrall, Director of Library and Information Services, Aston University, provided considerable guidance and the insight and advice which makes up this case study.

Mentoring can be viewed in two ways: as the icing on the cake for well managed, properly supported, highly motivated staff, or as a response to the identification of a particular need. Ideally, it will be part of a holistic approach to staff development which emphasizes participation, continuous improvement and personal responsibility. Mentoring ought to complement rather than supplant line management relationships, and it is therefore important to ensure that the latter are properly defined and in place before introducing such a scheme within an organization. Librarianship is a profession, and librarians can thus justify time invested in mentoring relationships as part of their contribution to the wider professional community.

Sheila Corrall has mentored people, and has been mentored, throughout her career, mainly on an informal basis. Her experience reflects the various roles identified by Mumford[8] – godfather, sponsor, guide, peer pal, and role model – and also described by the women featured in *Equally good.*[9] For those protégés whom she has sponsored, she has been able to job-spot, facilitating career moves by making connections between people and opportunities, offering to act as a referee, advise on applications and discuss long-term aspirations. She has acted as a counsellor through redundancy and organizational change, as a sounding board, and a proactive source of information on professional issues and concerns. At best there are similar interests, and a two-way process develops with substantial input from both mentor and protégé.

Sheila Corrall has found that age and gender are not significant, especially in those relationships where a friendship is established. Over the years this type of mentoring develops and benefits both people, and there may even be a reversal of roles if personal circumstances change.

2.12.1 Essential ingredients for successful mentoring

1 Keeping in touch
This is easier in the academic community where the availability of E-Mail enables frequent communication without the potentially disruptive effect of telephone calls during the working day. Maintaining regular contact demonstrates interest, facilitates exchange of information (for example about job applications), and reinforces the mentor's role in offering timely and sympathetic feedback.

2 First steps
Regular, frequent (ideally at least monthly) face-to-face meetings are essential in the early stages: a meeting over lunch or dinner often provides a suitable environment.

3 Line managers
Good line managers will fulfil many of the identified mentoring roles. However, a separate mentor can bring more objectivity to discussions: the mentor can stand back and will not have the same investment in the success of day-to-day projects. The mentor must take care not to undermine the line management relationship.

4 'People people'
You must be a people person to mentor successfully. It is essential to enjoy working with people, to be able to spot their positive qualities and abilities, and to have a strong sense of equity and fairness. Patience is essential.

2.12.2 Areas to watch out for

1 Ground rules
Sheila Corrall has not found the need to establish ground rules as she finds that protégés are generally responsible, and respectful of her time and availability. Some structure to the relationship is essential if mentoring is being pursued more formally, but it will constantly need re-appraising as the relationship develops. Mentoring through a specific project can create a heightened sense of demand, so the need and expectations require some attention when the project finishes. Mentoring usually starts off in a time of need and times of high need will be balanced by less intense periods. Career paths change and people switch directions so the mentoring relationship will alter and accommodate these fluctuations.

2 Barriers
In some cases the actual work-place can mitigate against the success of a participative management style which supports mentoring. Potential barriers include the size of the organization; people boxed into offices on several floors; and the existence of far-flung pockets of the organization. Managers need to be energetic and active to find the required effort to keep

in touch in such circumstances, and this can necessitate more structured and formal communication mechanisms.

2.12.3 Successful outcomes

Sheila Corrall considers that the greatest satisfaction gained from mentoring is when a mentor sees the successes and achievements of his/her protégé, which may be evidenced by a new post, a successful project, or simply the re-establishment of self-esteem and confidence. The recognition of talent, as well as the development of their own interpersonal skills, and their understanding of an individual, is also a source of fulfilment for mentors.

Sometimes they are compensating for other people's neglect, notably past or present line managers. A lack of visible achievements or outcomes can be demotivating. The establishment of learning objectives to set alongside an individual's service/task objectives can assist the development process by providing a focus for discussion, and enabling progress to be tracked via a series of milestones.

References

1　Darling, L. A. W., 'The mentoring discovery process: Helping people manage their mentoring', *Mentoring international*, **3** (2), 1989, 12–16.
2　Dodgson, J., 'Do women in education need mentors?', *Education Canada*, **Spring**, 1986, 29.
3　Phillips-Jones, L., *Mentors and protégés*, New York, Arbor House, 1982.
4　Burrington, G., 'Mentors – a source of skill, strength and enthusiasm', *Library Association record*, **95** (4), 1993, 226–7.
5　Carter, S., 'The development, implementation and evaluation of a mentoring scheme', *Industrial and commercial training*, **7**, July, 1994.
6　Roberts, D. L., 'Mentoring in the academic library', *College and research library news*, **February**, 1986, 117–19.
7　Ferriero, D. S., 'ARL directors as protégés and mentors', *Journal of academic librarianship*, **7** (6), 1982, 358–65.
8　Mumford, A., *Developing directors: the learning process*, London, Manpower Services Commission, 1987.
9　Burrington, G., *Equally good*, London, Association of Assistant Librarians, Limited, 1993.

3 The protégé

Who would want to be mentored and why?

David Clutterbuck[1] claims that everyone needs a mentor. Charles Handy[2] believes 'properly selfish' people will look for a mentor even before they are made wise by the experience of another. Finding a mentor is one way to provide for the lack of sufficient knowledge which may be identified as a restraining force if Trask[3] is being followed in any assessment of career planning. Mentoring is a way of learning, an aid to career planning, self-development and confidence building, and a way of achieving professional development.

It is necessary to have ambition or a will to succeed in order to put yourself in a position of being mentored. Apprenticeship is thought to be the concept which began the modern thinking behind mentoring. New entrants to a trade or profession needed the experience and knowledge which older individuals possessed. The following are the most general reasons for mentoring in the early stages of a career:

1   To assist in familiarizing new recruits with a particular organization while following the induction programme.[4]
2   To assist while working towards professional qualifications and preparing a professional development report. (The Association of Assistant Librarians' (AAL) Registration Liaison officers form a network which a professional development report writer may wish to contact in order to obtain support for this particular stage of career progression.)
3   To develop a mature attitude to management, while accepting increased responsibility in the fast tracks of library management training. (Mentoring allows this development in a more relaxed and natural way by providing the assistance of those already established.)

3.2 The learning experience

It is generally accepted that structured learning accounts for 20% of our actual knowledge whereas experiential learning can contribute a far greater proportion: 80%. It is important to combine both, but given the resources which are put into the structured area it is difficult to establish a priority for the larger and less structured area. If an organization establishes itself as a learning organization it must be prepared not only to promote learning but also to review the way in which it responds to events. Libraries which are currently undergoing change or transition could well employ this technique. Mentoring would have the effect of underpinning the learning which employees should be encouraged to undertake. Their own personal development and the organization will benefit from this initiative.

3.3 The learning organization

The learning organization was mooted by Kolb[5] and has been promoted by both Charles Handy[2] and Senge.[6] The application of a model for learning is the same for an organization as it is for an individual. It is about finding out the answers and not just knowing them; it is to learn from others and establish an individual way of solving a particular problem. There are no model answers in personal development and the presence of a mentor in one's career development does not mean an individual can abdicate from the responsibility for decision-making, but that one should learn from the process of problem solving.

3.4 The learning process

The process of learning is critical to mentoring; those subjecting themselves to the process must show a willingness to learn. Charles Handy[2] describes learning as a wheel which revolves around the need to question and solve problems by testing possible solutions or theories. Like any planning cycle there is a review period and it is within this period of reflection that the learning becomes complete and change can happen.

An individual may have a personality which encourages him/her to identify with a particular section of this wheel of learning: the questioner, who will be happiest raising the problems for others to solve; the pragmatist or activist, who will prefer to test the solutions; the theorist, who will happily work out answers for others to test; and the reflector, who will apply information to the success or otherwise of the outcomes. Mentors have to combine all parts of this wheel, and in addition have to encourage their protégés to do likewise if they are to achieve real learning from their problem situations. According to Mumford[7] the cycle is only effective when it has come full turn. The empirical experience it deals with means that until it has fully turned, the cycle must be completed before a true learning experience has occurred. The establishment of **learning objectives** in the mentor/protégé relationship may assist in the identification of a whole learning experience.

3.5 Mentoring in mid-career

Those in middle management may feel that the advice of a senior manager will assist them as they approach the final stages in management development. This is particularly true as people take on extra responsibilities, change post, or accept promotions which take them into different areas of operations. Women and minority groups can take advantage of a mentoring system and use it to ensure their networks are complete.

Alan Mumford[7] made some insightful comments about the development of managers in his work *Developing directors*. The best basis for management development, he suggests, is managerial work. The situations offered in reality provide a far more successful learning experience than any constructed 'classroom' techniques undertaken in MBA courses. If these experiences are undertaken with the assistance and advice of a mentor prior to the 'real thing', then the learning process will be enhanced further by the greater range of options being examined by the manager.

Being mentored also requires the protégé to focus attention on the way relationships are formed, and to apply judgement on whether or not they are successful. The ability to judge one's success in forming a good working relationship with a mentor, (which involves criticism as well as praise), is a valuable insight into the way in which one operates in the working environment. The process of examining the way the relationship works will highlight any further improvement or development in interpersonal skills.

3.6 Career planning

Career planning has been seen traditionally as a matter of personal responsibility. However, Sir Len Peach[8] argues that organizations should also take a share of this responsibility. During the early stages, and between the ages of 50-60, individuals will benefit from independent advice, and the organization will also be able to take advantage of this in terms of succession planning, and opening up opportunities to allow more flexible appointments to be made.

The introduction of the Continuing Professional Development profile by The Library Association is a valuable asset in career planning. This profile comprises a folder of worksheets for completion by the owner. It creates a picture of an individual in his/her career and other aspirations, and can be useful to anyone intending to develop a mentoring relationship. It is designed to allow for a full exploration of strengths and weaknesses, and as a record of achievement, logging all significant activities in an individual's professional life. The idea behind it was to establish a positive connection between personal and professional areas of activity, and by this holistic approach to a person's life, it shows the contributions, rather than the conflicts, which a variety of activities can provide.

The Institute of Manpower Studies at the University of Sussex include mentoring in a course on career planning. Designed for those interested in the concepts of self-development, or actively engaged in career workshops and development centres, the course offers mentoring as an example of a technique which can usefully be employed in the promotion of individual career planning.

Maria Burke[9] examines the introduction of student assessment of the learning experiences at Manchester Polytechnic (sic) through a career development report. This included the availability of a staff member to provide guidance and support for students. This was refined after the first year of implementation to use the student's personal tutor for the career development report. Once this type of discipline is accepted, it is easy to transfer the habit to the working environment, and use of the Professional Development Framework. The use of a mentor to guide a new professional through the professional maze will be a great advantage.

3.7 Personal development

Both professional and personal development can be helped enormously by the presence of mentors. Eleven interviewees in *Equally good* by Gill Burrington[10] acknowledge that they have been mentored at some point in their career, and two offer the benefits which they have found in mentoring others. The next section uses the evidence of these librarians to illustrate the way mentoring can assist both professional and personal development.

3.7.1 Confidence

This is often missing in the new professional.

Ziggi Alexander[10] offers the most lyrical and inspirational advice which she obtained from an older black woman professional: 'Learn to be the centre of your universe. You will then be a powerful black woman instead of pretending to be one.' Peggy Smith[10] is candid in acknowledging that it was the openness about her strengths and weaknesses with a senior manager which enabled the confidence in her own abilities to be established and maintained.

3.8 Professional development

3.8.1 Organizational protocol

A protégé will encounter many situations in which a basic understanding of the organization is necessary in order to ensure the best outcome. It is this crucial information which is often missing. Sandra Parker[10] maintains that it can be provided by someone with knowledge of, and access to, the critical information about the organization. This can be done in an unthreatening way, creating an environment where 'waters can be tested' without commitment.

3.8.2 Specialist areas

It can be difficult to choose a particular area in which to make your mark. Professions are multi-faceted and often very different areas prove to be attractive. Mentors are quoted as the catalyst which new professionals need to 'fire their enthusiasm' in a particular area. Carol Banks, Grace Kempster, and Peggy Smith are all recorded in *Equally good* by Gill Burrington,[10] as having found that their managers were people who were enthusiasts about services to children and young people. They were allowed to experiment with responsibility, under the watchful and critical eye of their manager.

3.8.3 Common interests

A protégé needs to find someone who shares the same sense of joy in the areas of common concern. Liz Weir[10] was surprised to find that the whole new world of childrens' literature could be opened up to her by someone who was influential, but who was prepared to share the excitement of the subject with a group of new professionals.

3.8.4 Experience

To have those in influential positions offering valuable insight into the range of decision-making situations can be resented. Sandra Ward[10] disapproved of opportunities which were only available to those who knew someone influential. Patronage is not the same as mentoring and the introduction of formal mentoring does allow for a more equal treatment of new professionals or other group, selected to benefit from the scheme.

3.8.5 Commitment

In Equally good, Gill Burrington[10] makes the comment that mentors can make a considerable difference to a career, and the commitment which one can make to the development of the service in which one is employed. Within the cases described in this book, there is a shared pride and value in the professional commitment expressed. Thus it is easy to establish a high correlation between success and the presence of mentors in a career.

3.9 Protégé training

Anyone who is being mentored should prepare for the process in the same way as they would for appraisal. It will do justice to the training to which mentors are committing themselves, and will be good preparation for a number of other activities which are bound to occur throughout a career.

3.9.1 Personal SWOT analysis

Preparation for the protégé will include an examination of personal strengths and weaknesses, opportunities and threats. **Strengths** will include current skills and qualifications. Identifying **weaknesses** will mean an honest listing of the areas known to need attention, and knowledge which must be gained, in order to achieve the aims set. **Opportunities** may not be tangible; they may only exist as a 'wish list' of aspirations, while **threats** may not be real either but rather an individual's perceptions of barriers to the career success which they hope for.

The Henley mentoring kit (See Appendix C) includes a SWOT analysis for completion in one of the stages of the mentor process. Individuals should know their own strengths, weaknesses, opportunities and threats before they enter into the examination of them by another.

Knowing oneself is a vital part of the honesty which is necessary in the mentor and protégé relationship. The advantage of this early examination will also mean that areas for improvement will have been acknowledged before a mentor draws attention to them.

3.9.2 Organizational SWOT

As well as examining personal strengths and weaknesses it will be necessary for the protégé to pay some attention to the organization. Looking critically at the organization does not mean listing what is wrong with it. It is more a systematic examination of the way it works, and the identification of the gaps in personal knowledge, so that they can be filled in at some future date.

Important areas to examine are the staffing structure, the decision-making process, and the organization chart. Correlations between these three areas should be made, and from that, an understanding of the organization will begin to emerge.

3.9.3 Personal aspirations

Personal aspirations in one's career or profession should be identified. Any new employee will need to identify the organization's mission, aims and objectives. A mentor is in a position of strength to guide a new employee towards the correlation of organizational aims and objectives with personal aspirations.

3.9.4 Skills

If not already listed in a Curriculum Vitae (CV), a protégé should outline his/her skills and competences. Those currently possessed, and those required to fulfil the personal, career or professional objectives should be listed. A protégé who is already using The Library Association's Continuing Professional Development (CPD) Framework will have already completed much of this task.

3.10 Skills to develop at the outset

The ability to communicate in an articulate manner is essential in all areas of interaction with others and not just with the mentor. The creation of opportunities to practise accurate descriptions of circumstances and feelings about certain situations, is good skills training. It is always beneficial to rehearse and practise, and so much better to do this in the presence of someone who is committed to the success of one's ventures.

A realistic understanding of the mentor relationship will require a protégé to put considerable intellectual effort into understanding the process. Reasonable demands are likely to be met with equal reason, but expectations must not exceed the responsibilities of the 'contract'.

The shared responsibility which the protégé and the mentor have for the success of the relationship depends upon the input to which both are committed. It is not acceptable to expect the mentor to solve the problems. His/her role here is to facilitate the understanding of the problems in order to find an acceptable solution. The exact nature of this role cannot be dictated, but ground rules for both partners should be articulated and understood.

3.11 Documentation

It may be helpful to have some sample documents to use in establishing the mentoring relationship. The suggestions given are based on the available literature, principally the Henley mentoring kit (see Appendix C).

3.11.1 Contract

This will state the names of the parties to be involved in the mentoring arrangement, the commitment to the particular type of development for which the arrangement is made, and may indicate the 'ground rules' which apply. There may be some reference to the method by which this will be achieved, and to agreed learning objectives meeting career or development objectives. It should suggest ways in which it is anticipated that these goals or objectives may be reached. The document should be clear in its purpose and signed by both parties.

3.11.2 SWOT analysis

A personal SWOT analysis will indicate current strengths, personal areas which need development (weaknesses), career aspirations (opportunities), and perceived obstacles or restrictions (threats). See 3.9.1 above.

3.11.3 Expectations list

This acts rather like a 'pros and cons' list. It is necessary to examine motives before setting out on this course of action. It is also realistic to examine one's expectations before exploring their realization with one's mentor.

3.11.4 Action plan

Both parties will find themselves agreeing to certain actions before the next meeting. It is far better to write these down and agree the timetable for their implementation, than hope that memory alone will provide the motivation for action.

3.12 Protégé case study

These reflections from a protégé are based not only on personal experience but also on the wider experience of others who took part in a pilot scheme at Staffordshire University.

'What was so good was that she was always on my side, and she always saw my point of view.' This quote was from an assistant librarian who was a protégé in a successful mentoring relationship which was established as part of a pilot mentoring scheme, devised for women at Staffordshire University under the Opportunity 2000 scheme. This scheme was additional to, but recognized as complementary to, staff appraisal, and dealt with the personal and not the professional or job-related development of individuals who took part as protégés.

Staffordshire University Professional Womens' Development Network committed themselves to the introduction of a one year pilot of a mentoring scheme in 1992. Under the direction of Pro-Vice Chancellor Dr Christine King, and organized by Maureen Atkinson, Head of Professional Womens' Development Network at the University, the scheme was devised to assist the development of every woman who wished to take part, wherever employed, and on all conditions of service, part-time or full-time, clerical, domestic or professional staff - women employees being seen to be at some disadvantage to their male counterparts in university staffing structures.

A meeting of all those interested, at all levels, was held and from this, names of those wishing to participate as mentors or protégés were established. Interviews were held to progress the matching process, and a third person was to be available to assist the initial meeting.

Following a process of allocation carried out by the organizers, the pairs were given a wide brief to establish the ground rules for their own mentoring relationships. A member of the library staff was successfully paired with a member of university personnel, previously known to her. There was a freedom on both parts to agree to this particular pairing.

The scheme took a practical rather than theoretical approach, and a minimum of paperwork accompanied the introduction of the process. It was described as a 'let's stop talking and get going' initiative. No formal documentation was available, and the meeting frequency and location were matters of joint negotiation and agreement. Both parties provided an agenda for the first meeting, and agreement was reached on the format and location of future meetings.

The scheme was to last for six months. The two parties paced themselves well, and their mentoring meetings achieved a great deal in the time span allotted. The meetings have continued but are now less formal and take place in 'free' time, often over lunch.

The protégé's reason for wanting to be mentored arose from a perceptive realization that the library seemed isolated from much of the general business of the university. This is especially true for those at site libraries away from the administrative heart of the organization. There is a very real perception that the business of the university takes place in the schools or departments, and that the library is rarely the place of dynamic activity, central to the heart of the aims and objectives of the organization.

The protégé in this case needed a context to her work, an understanding of the structure and the work of the committees, a knowledge of 'who people were' and how it all 'fitted together'. The mentor was able to explain this, and to introduce the protégé to a considerable number of other people within the organization.

Encouragement was given to the protégé to take part in other university initiatives, and this was particularly successful as the initiative selected provided an opportunity to receive further training in counselling and listening techniques.

The protégé's personal ambition is reflected in her decision to seek a mentor, as is frequent in self-motivated individuals. From it, she has gained an insight into the organization, enabling her to be more confident in her dealings with a variety of library users.

The mentor in this case was well placed to provide an overview of the organization, to introduce her to a network of individuals and to provide learning opportunities connected with and complementary to her work. She assisted by sharing additional resources in the form of tapes and videos for use with certain situations, all of which enabled the protégé to grow in skill and confidence.

Communications with all those involved were not always made. While senior managers (especially if they were women) knew about the scheme, it was possible for some managers to be unaware of the initiative. Line managers usually knew, as the participants were encouraged to meet within the work-place and in work time. Although introduced from the top (at second-level management in this case), the scheme did not cover the whole organization and some guilt/resentment was experienced by those whose managers were not fully involved.

The allocation of a senior person did cause some more 'junior' staff to feel in awe, and unable to take the first step towards initiating the mentoring relationship. Neither did all mentors embrace this vital first stage, thus allowing the protégé to feel they were accessible and available to them.

No training was given to mentors, and no guidance to protégés. This had detrimental effects on some mentoring relationships, where both parties acknowledged that it was a good thing, but neither really knew where to start in defining the future structure of this relationship.

Geographical location was also a factor, when mentors were paired with protégés who worked at a distant site. There was no interference with the various mentoring partnerships which were part of the pilot, and for those where there were no problems, this was 'fine'. However, there was no monitoring either, and if nothing was happening, there was no-one to take responsibility for getting things back on track. However, some evaluation of the pilot scheme has been carried out, and Staffordshire University intend to carry on offering the scheme as a development tool for women. Mentors can be either men or women.

For this protégé the outcome was a positive boost to a new and promising career. There is a commitment to mentor in the future, and to enable another new employee to become part of the larger organization. The whole experience was described in positive terms and was deemed to be a success.

References

1 Clutterbuck, D., *Everyone needs a mentor*, (2nd edn.), London, IPM, 1991.
2 Handy, C., *The age of unreason*, London, Arrow, 1990.
3 Trask, M. and Wood, J., *Career planning and assessment for librarians*, Lindfield, N.S.W., College of Advanced Education, 1984.
4 Parry, J., *Induction*, London, Library Association Publishing Limited, 1993.
5 Kolb, D. and Fry, R., 'Towards an applied theory of experiential learning', in Cooper, C. L. (ed.), *Theories of group process*, Chichester, Wiley, 1975.
6 Senge, P.M., *The fifth discipline: the art and practice of the learning organisation*, (*sic*) New York, Doubleday Currency, 1990.
7 Mumford, A., *Developing directors: the learning process*, London, Manpower Services Commission, 1987.
8 Peach, L., 'Planning careers', *Personnel today*, **23 November**, 1993, 15.
9 Burke, M. E., 'Career development report: one perspective', *Personnel, training and education*, **9** (3), 1992, 76–7.
10 Burrington, G., *Equally good*, London, Association of Assistant Librarians, 1993.

Skills and qualities for the mentor

4.1 Introduction

John Carruthers[1] refers to 'natural mentors', but it is debatable whether such persons exist. That we can recognize the qualities which we believe would make someone a good mentor or leader is due to the presence of a high level of competence in the core skills which we understand are necessary for the roles of a mentor (see 2.3) to be fulfilled.

The skills which mentors need are reflected in the roles which they play in the process of mentoring. Mentors need to be able to **assess needs**, to **counsel** and to **negotiate**. In order to be successful in these roles, the mentor must have confidence in his/her **communication** skills.

As well as skills, a mentor needs certain **qualities** and **characteristics**. These can be put together to form a profile, although the uniqueness of any mentoring relationship will alter the profile. Eric Parsloe[2] provides the background to the development of a mentor, but fails to articulate what the profile looks like.

A mentor will need a set of **core skills**. These skills are interrelated and may already be present in individuals who are contemplating becoming mentors. The decision to become a mentor is a serious one, and individuals will have assessed their own competence before the final step is taken. Therefore, one must assume the presence of **interpersonal skills** (see Levy[3]), **communication**, and **analytical skills** in an 'intending' mentor. This does not negate the need for additional training according to individual needs (see Williamson[4]). Programmes should be devised so that opportunities occur for those contemplating mentoring, and not just for those who have decided to become mentors.

The confirmation of skills is an important factor in building the confidence which mentors must have in their ability. Whatever the skills, there must also be a display of competence in them. The Institution of Industrial Managers' Leader series has been established for management students, and the programmes are designed to integrate learning opportunities at work with the theoretical elements of management training. Mentoring exists between someone within the company and an IIM student, and thus complements the traditional tutor/student relationship for the college-based work.

Burrington[5] and Parsloe[2] offer guidance in the basic skills required of mentors, while Wilkin[6] gives the specific skills required of those mentoring students engaged in school-based training for the teaching profession. Librarians will need these core skills, for they do not change whatever the form of mentoring used.

4.2   Core skills

4.2.1   Communication

Listening is the most vital of all the skills of communication. However good the presentation, it is meaningless unless someone hears, and understands what is being said. Being able to extract the essence of what is said, and to interpret it as the speaker intended, is not as simple as listening. Chinese whispers! Also important is **how** something is said. To be able to detect the strain in someone's voice, to identify emotion or confidence, one must be able to interpret the tone or the volume level used in speech. All these signals will offer mentors an opportunity to formulate a thoroughly competent response, and enable them to offer a constructive reply to the protégé.

4.2.2   Effective or active listening

This needs practice. Because we speak at a pace four times slower than the brain can process the words, we have spare mental capacity when we are listening. If a mentor allows his/her mind to wander when listening to a point made by a protégé, there is a danger of destroying some of the trust which is essential for the relationship to succeed. One should not contemplate mentoring if one not only finishes peoples' sentences, but also provides the end of their questions for them.

The skill of listening is shown by a person's ability to paraphrase or repeat what has been said in a way which confirms the protégé's meaning. This is also a way to elicit more information, which will help in the next stage of listening.

4.3   Analytical skills

4.3.1   Interpretation

In order to make an informed response, the listener needs to digest what has been said. This will lead to better understanding and to the next stage of the process.

4.3.2   Creative thinking

In *The professional decision-thinker* Ben Heirs and Peter Farrell[7] invite readers to examine the way they think when making decisions. To some, the challenges to accepted patterns of thinking will be as taxing as learning a new language. Creative thinking is necessary for mentors, who will need to absorb another's thinking process, and thus unblock some of their own **mind sets**. The ability to think divergently and to include optional answers to questions which a protégé may pose, is another skill which must be acquired and practised. Creative thinking requires individuals to adopt an imaginative and an intuitive approach, to consider alternative answers to a problem and to take more time over the evaluation of a problem. A mentor will need to challenge the immediate reactions of a protégé. In order to justify this, mentors will need to have considered the various solutions themselves, compensating in some way for the inexperience of the protégé.

As with Charles Handy's[8] learning organization, there is a model for creative decision thinking. The four stages are:

- The question
- The alternatives
- The consequences
- The decision.

Note the use of the plural in stages two and three.

4.3.3 Evaluation

Evaluation of information requires the application of knowledge and experience, as well as familiarity with the situation, and necessitates identification of the real issues. 'Seeing the wood for the trees' will allow the mentor to respond appropriately to the protégé. The mentor's analysis is a critical factor in the evaluation process.

4.4 Interpersonal skills

4.4.1 Observation

A mentor must be able to interpret behaviour accurately. He/she must be aware of body language, facial expressions, tone of voice, be sensitive to language used and indeed to the need to temper language, though not so much that the personality changes. Behaviour can change when a person's work or actions are under scrutiny. A mentor will need to develop a sensitivity to behavioural changes in the protégé, and an ability to be accurate in his/her assessment of what is said and what is meant.

4.4.2 Questioning

The ability to ask questions which will take the protégé into areas of self-exploration of the situation is essential. These questions must be structured and meaningful. The interviewing skills of asking open and direct questions, and offering prompts without leading the conversation, must be developed. The process of questioning (which leads into the understanding of the problem by the protégé) is the most rewarding situation for the mentor in the early stages of a mentoring relationship.

4.5 Applying the skills

The mentor must identify the facts as well as the emotions behind a situation. Listening accurately and observing all the signals is essential. Glib, cliché-ridden responses are most unhelpful, as they will undermine the protégé's confidence and indicate that his/her needs are not being taken seriously. Assessment of needs is therefore a process of applying the interpersonal skills, particularly those of observation and listening, and then communicating them in an appropriate and acceptable way to the protégé.

4.5.1 Assessment of needs

One measure of the value of a mentor/protégé relationship will be found by establishing the similarity of experience and assessment of needs. The mentor will still also have needs, but will have experienced more of those same needs and their satisfaction than the protégé articulates.

Although each individual has a unique set of needs, the mentor who can empathize and identify with the protégé stands a greater chance of assessing successfully the needs of that person as they move from a problem to its solution.

4.5.2 Counselling

This requires the mentor to identify correctly the situation or problem, and to illustrate to the protégé how they can control it. In some cases the actual situation has not been recognized by the protégé, and the mentor has to guide and identify without the protégé feeling inadequate. The next stage of counselling is to take the protégé through possible outcomes, and to enable him/her to make an informed decision. The final stage requires action to effect any change in the situation. At all times control must remain with the protégé. It is their situation, their decision and their outcome. Mentoring is enabling, not instructing.

4.5.3 Negotiation

Mentoring is a continual process. Therefore, the action required of a mentor may result in the need to extend the relationship beyond the one established with the protégé. In formal systems of mentoring, some form of feedback to others who are instrumental in the development of the protégé will be necessary. There will be occasions when the mentor has to discuss the needs analysis which they have made of the protégé with the line manager or others in the development/training departments. Negotiation implies that some amount of persuasion will be required, and that compromise may have to be achieved. The skills of negotiation can therefore require conflict management as tension in situations must be dealt with. This may arise through personality clashes, as well as differences in interpretations of the situation. Training for negotiation is an imperative.

4.5.4 Dealing with conflict

A mentor must know how to pre-empt conflict, how to recognize the early stages and how to take avoiding action. Occasions may arise when the mentor may find the protégé's analysis of his/her situation naïve and certainly the protégé may feel resentful of the mentor and his/her experience and achievements.

Being able to handle conflict and confrontation is a difficult skill to acquire, and women are often thought to be particularly vulnerable to the negative sides of conflict. To establish a position, and to give assertive justification for it, is necessary in many management situations. A good example, set within the trusting nature of the mentoring relationship, will indicate to the protégé how these situations can be resolved successfully.

It is not always possible to avoid conflict, and if it does arise, a mentor must be prepared to resolve it. The first step is to examine the stages which led up to the conflict, and to identify any previous indications that it was about to happen. Pin-pointing the exact nature of the conflict is important, so that the solution matches the problem; scapegoats are easy to present and can mask the real root of the difficulty. The reasons for the conflict must be elicited from the protégé, and listening skills must be employed. A summary of possible actions and reasons for them should then be given, and the protégé should be encouraged to agree to a specific course of action to rectify the position.

4.5.5 Timing

It is helpful if a timetable is established in these difficult situations. Vague agreement 'to do it sometime' can indicate a lack of acceptance of the action, and it may not happen. To show support and confidence in the protégé's ability to take the action is critical to the relationship. It must be articulated and not implied or taken as read. It is in respect of such critical matters that relationships succeed or fail.

4.5.6 Offering feedback

Mentoring depends on the giving and receiving of feedback and criticism. This is another extremely hard skill to acquire, for it requires an honesty which may be hurtful to an inexperienced person. Feedback must be constructive; comments which cannot usefully be incorporated into the protégé's future work are not justified.

4.6 Qualities

We should not underestimate the positive qualities which a mentor will need. There are many skills which are desirable, but without a sensitivity to the process they will be difficult to apply.

4.6.1 Understanding

This concept is complicated by the necessity not only to understand, but also to ensure that the protégé understands.

4.6.2 Thoughtfulness

This is a quality required of mentors. The ability to offer time, **uninterrupted** time, by diverting phone calls and placing notices on office doors so that any sessions are not disturbed, is essential. It is necessary to understand the cultural behaviour acceptable to the protégé, and this can alter if the mentor and protégé do not share a common background.

4.6.3 Sensitivity to setting

Mentors must be aware of the interpretations which may be made about body language. They should accept that some protégés will need more physical space to feel at ease. An honest approach and friendly openness and a willingness to concede to requests for particular seating arrangements or locations, should be adopted in the interests of achieving success. It is important to acknowledge that eye contact and the different meanings which can be conveyed at the same time by verbal and non-verbal signals, may be interpreted in a particular way, especially by those unused to such a situation. At the same time, it is important to be natural and not self-conscious. Practice should enhance this particular skill.

4.6.4 Lack of prejudice

De-prejudice yourself! It is easy to be trapped by accents and dress, in addition to the unacceptable prejudices of age, race and sex. Everyone is liable to misjudge certain situations or people at some time. A skilled mentor will be able to pre-empt this happening in the mentoring situation and will be aware of their own prejudices even if they have not eradicated them.

4.6.5 Enthusiasm

It is doubtful if anyone can be a successful mentor without enthusiasm. A joy in people and their achievements will stem from a confidence and maturity of outlook. Having chosen a profession and enjoyed it, it is easy to impart that feeling to others.

4.6.6 Confidence building

Building confidence requires facing the negative aspects, as well as capitalizing on the positive areas of one's personality. Talking about oneself is very difficult for some people and mentors must appreciate this fact. Natural reticence, or learned modesty, can mean an unsuccessful articulation of an individual's good points. When a protégé faces failure the mentor can provide the encouragement and motivation required to make the next positive step. It is at this stage that offering ideas is vital. Offering help once a course of action has been identified by the protégé is appropriate; taking control and doing it for them is not.

4.6.7 Insight

This is partly analysis and understanding, and partly intelligent application of those skills which allow the right judgement to be made about the situation, and the relevant options available to individuals. Parsloe[2] considers that a mentor must understand why mentoring is different from any of the other roles which one plays.

Knowledge of what it takes to be a good mentor will guide many to an appropriate understanding of how to undertake the role. One of the most beneficial insights that any mentor will be expected to anticipate is when the relationship has run its natural course, and achieved all the aims and objectives set. This requires both insight and tact, and is not unlike the understanding which parents must achieve if their children are to go out into the world and attain independence.

4.7 Summary

Any person wishing to become a mentor for another must first understand the essential skills which are required for the various roles which may be required. By assessing the skills needed, potential mentors can examine their strengths and weaknesses, and attend to the skills training which should be undertaken.

Skills are only the first step, as there are qualities which a mentor exhibits which must also be acquired. This stage of becoming a mentor is the hardest, as it needs a particular kind of personality to accept that a protégé may behave differently from oneself in any situation. The accommodation of different views and reactions can result in conflict, which must be handled without the situation becoming personal. The qualities of honesty and integrity, coupled with good communication skills, will take potential mentors a long way forward in their training.

References

1 Caldwell, B. J. and Carter, E. M. A., *Return of the mentor*, London, Falmer Press, 1993.
2 Parsloe, E., *Coaching, mentoring and assessing: a practical guide to developing competence*, London, Kogan Page, 1992.
3 Levy, P., *Interpersonal skills*, London, Library Association Publishing Limited, 1993.
4 Williamson, M., *Training needs analysis*, London, Library Association Publishing Limited, 1993.
5 Burrington, G., 'On being a mentor', *Course programme for The Library Association Continuing Education Department*, 30 September 1993 and 8 February 1994.
6 Wilkin, M., *Mentoring in schools*, London, Kogan Page, 1992.
7 Heirs, B. and Farrell, P., *The professional decision-thinker*, London, Grafton, 1989.
8 Handy, C., *The age of unreason*, London, Arrow 1990.

5 The formal mentoring system

5.1 Introduction

This chapter deals with mentoring schemes which organizations may wish to establish for a group or groups of protégés. It is not necessary to establish informal mentoring relationships in this way: see Chapter 6 for further comment in this context. Introducing a formalized mentoring system provides an opportunity for a full acknowledgement of the time and commitment to personal development which mentors offer.

If an organization introduces mentoring, it is underlining its own philosophy as a learning organization, providing a forum for mentoring to happen, and enabling personal objectives to coincide with organizational objectives in a critical area of staff development.

If an organization is to introduce mentoring, the system needs to be structured and documented, and there will be specific aims and objectives. Short-term, this can be for induction or management 'grooming' purposes, but long-term, it will be for reasons which will include **'succession planning'**. Some organizations will use mentoring in order to identify individuals who have management potential.

5.2 The players

This LTG has discussed the two main people in the mentoring formula, though it should be remembered that in most organizations, the line manager will also feature in the equation. As it has been emphasized, mentoring is not training, but formal mentoring may have resource consequences. If the organization has a training officer, he/she will need to be aware of the outcomes of mentoring if these result in training requirements. There will also be an interaction between appraisal and mentoring schemes which will highlight the line manager's responsibilities, and provide a further link with the training officer.

5.2.1 The protégé

Chapter 3 has fully described those who would benefit from mentoring by becoming a protégé.

5.2.2 The mentor

Chapter 2 has fully described the mentor's role.

5.2.3 The line manager

The line manager must be a partner in any mentor relationship. There may be occasions when the line manager identifies a situation where mentoring would provide a solution to a development problem in one of his/her staff. As mentors do not have sole responsibility for the protégé, the line manager will retain an essential role in the protégé's development. In organization-wide mentoring schemes, this partnership between the interested parties is crucial to the well-being of the protégé, and to the avoidance of confusion over roles, or conflict between individuals.

The line manager will be able to offer or reinforce training, and therefore learning opportunities. By being party to the development objectives, the line manager can focus the protégé's attention on the learning outcomes from the work undertaken.

5.2.4 The training officer

The training officer or other personnel specialist may take the role of programme co-ordinator. In this case, the vital role of the training officer is to communicate, and act as an interpreter of the system, where the main individuals fail to comprehend it.

In organizations which introduce mentoring, the training department should oversee the training needs of those acting as mentors. The department will adopt a role defined by the parent organization, in accordance with the philosophy chosen for staff development. Some organizations will require active monitoring, particularly if they are concerned to quantify the benefits of mentoring.

Training officers will provide assistance to mentors in order to implement training or development needs which the protégé has which are beyond the responsibility of the immediate line manager.

5.2.5 Senior managers

There are many initiatives which will fail if they are not supported at the highest level. Mentoring systems are in danger if they are not introduced with top management support, and are part of a broader human resources strategy.

Other senior managers may be asked for advice in situations with which the mentor is less familiar, as for example other areas of the organization in which the protégé has expressed interest.

5.2.6 A note for all players

It is important that all parties have each others' confidence. Information about the nature of the decisions made by a protégé, in either the mentoring relationship or in line-management appraisal, must be treated with utmost confidence but have maximum effect. It would be unfortunate if barriers were created by the need for confidentiality, when opportunities for development needed to be explored by consultation between mentor and line manager. A protocol for such consultation will help to eliminate confusion.

5.3 The organization

The organization itself is a participant, in the sense that there must be agreement throughout about the value of mentoring, or any other development tool, as applied to the employees. An organization contemplating mentoring will have one or more of the following objectives:

1 To ensure that the needs of management in the future are taken care of (succession planning).

2 To avoid promotions for the 'wrong' reasons.

3 To eliminate élitism and exclusivity amongst new recruits, some of whom will be sufficiently assertive to establish themselves with the influential members of an organization's senior management.

4 To ensure the application of equal opportunity policies for all new employees.

5 To promote a corporate identity or cultural change.

6 To increase staff morale or decrease staff turnover.

5.4 The characteristics of organizations introducing mentoring

1 They will be equal opportunity employers.

2 They will have committed themselves to staff development, and have provided resources in terms of time, finance and motivation.

3 They will wish to develop cost-effective methods of staff development.

4 They will actively seek to improve the internal communications network.

5 They will be learning organizations where professional development, self-development contracts, incidental or experiential learning are recognized.

6 They will wish to develop their services or markets by learning.

7 They will be caring organizations, as described by Charles Handy.[1] This definition is absent from books on organizational management, but Handy claims it should be a major feature contributing to a good working environment.

8 They will value the individual.

9 They will wish any risks taken to be the subject of informed decision-making, and not open to criticism if the initiative fails.

10 They will have a culture of excitement, question and experiment, exploration and adventure, not reigns of fear![1]

5.5 Organizational issues

The organization will need to address quite seriously the qualities it wants to cultivate. It will have to acknowledge the time and resources required to do it.

It cannot back out without notice. Once set up, mentoring will have to take its own course. The organization may not say that mentoring will become a matter of personal choice.

It will need to set up some form of review of the system (**not** of individual mentoring arrangements; these will have their own life span).

5.6 Introduction of the mentoring system

5.6.1 Analysis

In an interview with the author, Jenny Sweeney, an Industrial Society consultant, was quite clear about the need for organizations to examine their motives for introducing mentoring. Without some initial analysis there is a danger of introducing mentoring either for the wrong reasons or in an ill-considered way.

5.6.2　Purpose

The exact nature and purpose of the scheme must be clear to all. It will be necessary to identify who is to be mentored and what aims will be met by mentoring.

5.6.3　Role of the mentor

The organization must decide what they want the mentor to do. This will range from personal development, career development, or learning experience by 'placement'. The exact nature is not important; what is essential is that there is agreement.

5.6.4　Timescale

Having established a need for mentoring and commitment to it, a proper timescale for introduction should be established. The only rule should be not to rush ahead before an understanding has been reached by all involved. The proper time to introduce mentoring is when there is agreement by all parties about the realistic realization of expectations.

5.6.5　The contract

The result of the above will define the nature of the contract. Some form of written agreement is helpful to formalize the ground rules and code of conduct for the relationship. Other contract items could include the regularity of meetings, guidance on where meetings should take place, and any other agreements which mentor and protégé feel necessary.

5.6.6　Ground rules

These will be established in part by the organization, and in part by the two individuals. Some organizations like British Telecom insist that mentoring is carried on in a non-alcohol environment, in line with existing organization policy. Between the individuals, there will be issues of time, areas which are deemed 'off-limits' (especially private life), authorization of mentor with regard to the use of contacts and networks, and respect for the privileges which these bring. The protégé will require assurance that there will be no insistence or control exercised by the mentor, in order that they remain in charge of their own achievements.

5.6.7　Design of the system

It may be that the organization wishes to place this critical role into the hands of a consultant. The Industrial Society is an objective adviser in this area, and other management consultants may be approached to fulfil this role. If this is done in-house, the objectives of the organization will lead the design of the system, and the reason why mentoring is to be introduced will inform the objectives of the scheme. Having a staff development policy (see Parry) will assist this process, as the development objectives will already be outlined. Training needs can also lead the development and, as Williamson[3] indicates, this is a process which must distinguish between the genuine need and the personal wish, in order to establish clearly the precise training needs which will provide performance improvement.

5.6.8 Implementation

Like all planning exercises, mentoring will have a planning cycle aligned to that which the organization usually adopts as a framework for implementation. There must be time for the investigation of the validity of the scheme, the drawing up of the aims, objectives and monitoring systems, the initial introduction and accompanying preparation of documentation, and the induction process which provides the platform for the marketing of the initiative. These terms may sound clinical and inappropriate for something as personal as mentoring, but it must be remembered that mentoring is being introduced as a human resource development strategy, and that the organization is to benefit from the additional motivation and commitment which employees will obtain from it.

5.6.9 Selection of pairs

How people will be brought together is an important consideration. The main choices are natural mentors, sponsors or peer mentors. The use of line managers is not advised by Sweeney as indicated in her interview with the author of this guide. Other considerations at this stage will include gender; physical co-location of mentor and protégé; voluntary or mandatory nature of scheme; how many protégés a mentor should take on.

5.6.10 Training

Training in both skills and process should be offered to all mentors. In addition, line managers and protégés should receive an introduction and a briefing, in order to be properly equipped and aware of their responsibilities to each other and to themselves.

Training for mentors should include communication and interviewing techniques, identification and further development of the skills of mentoring, and how they 'fit' with the scheme which the organization is introducing.

There should be sessions for all involved on the nature and philosophy of the scheme, and how the achievements of mentoring will match the aims and objectives of the organization. The Industrial Society recommends at least one day with the mentor. The sessions should be planned in accordance with the scheme, but examples of mentor training sessions are to be found in Appendix C.

When mentoring is introduced, line-managers must be briefed by the trainer. This should include information about the mechanism whereby the line manager is informed about performance-related issues which the mentor discovers about the protégé, but without any betrayal of confidence.

The protégé should certainly be well informed about the system. For many, this will be the first experience of such a relationship, and they will need a chance to explore their own expectations of mentoring. There will be some ground work to be covered by the protégé, by way of an examination of strengths and weaknesses, identifying career objectives, enumerating skills and competences, and priorities for the future relationship with a senior member of the organization.

5.6.11 Resources

Time is perhaps the greatest resource which an organization must find if mentoring is to be successful. David Clutterbuck[4] suggests two questions which must be asked concerning the disruption to the normal work of both protégé and mentor, and the assessment of the value of the time and effort involved in developing the protégé. As most mentors will be senior people, they must be freed to commit themselves to the needs of their protégés. New employees may find it difficult to request time to meet their mentor, but if the Miami-Dade example (see 5.9) is used, it can be seen that the mentor becomes responsible for the protégé while they are with them, and that the learning which they receive from mentors is part of the process of induction required for any employee to make a full contribution.

5.6.12   Monitoring

Monitoring an initiative such as mentoring can be a problem. There are no easy and accessible standards against which success can be measured. Communication with all parties is one way of reminding them that mentoring is taking place, why it is being done and how it fits in with other staff development activities (see Hamilton[5]).

5.6.13   Evaluation and review

The responsible mentor will of course monitor the progress of the protégé. Evaluation of their own activities is also necessary if a return is to be assessed by the organization. It is helpful to new mentors if they are provided with an outline of the issues which protégés can expect to have covered over a specific length of time. The Miami-Dade case study (see 5.9) offers some examples of the type of situation which a mentor should expect to include in a typical programme for a protégé in higher education. This can be adapted and integrated with the induction programme so that they complement each other.

The development of the relationships will need some assessment after an agreed interval. This should be on a regular basis, though preferably not at the time of the appraisal interviews, or it will be inextricably linked with that process. Hamilton[5] suggests two or three times every year with both mentors and protégés. However much emphasis is placed on altruism, it cannot be denied that any organization should primarily be interested in improving its performance, and maintaining a high quality service ethos. This is especially true in library and information services.

The existence of standards or measurements will also indicate the level of operation expected of an employee. Thus the mentor, with his/her longer experience of the organization, will be better able to guide the protégé towards the required level or standard of performance. This knowledge is critical to the progress of a new employee, and not something which is found in a job description.

5.7   What are the benefits of mentoring?

The Industrial Society has now completed two surveys on the use of mentoring in British business.[6,7] The results reported show an increase in uptake of this particular system of staff development. However, there is no British data on mentoring in libraries which can be used to provide objective support for this initiative.

If an organization wishes to quantify the returns on investment in training and development, a schedule will need to be established for the measurements and the **benchmarks** which form the starting point for the measurements. By using the levels of competence established for the library and information profession by the National Vocational Qualifications, a manager will be able to assess value added, or additional performance of a member of staff, when they are participating in a mentoring scheme.

Performance levels establish the performance targets for training. A mentor will be able to guide a protégé towards and beyond these levels, and this assessment will provide a performance measure, which will enable the senior managers to see the returns on their investment in the process and system of mentoring.

With a monitoring system in place, the effectiveness of the organization can be measured, and improvements can be attributed to the changes which have been introduced. In a non-exploitative way, it will complement an individual's progress and increased personal effectiveness in the work. One of the most comprehensive examinations of measuring returns is provided by Earl Carter.[8]

5.7.1　Improved quality

One of the important features of introducing mentoring is the way in which it can improve the quality of the organization. This is a feature which many American organizations use in their literature on mentoring.

5.8　What can go wrong?

Difficulties which can be attributed to inexperience are not unusual. Often the protégé does not understand the reactions which his/her activities provoke in other people. The mentor's role is to make their protégés more aware of their personal impact on others. However, there are certain danger signals which a mentor must be able to recognize.

5.8.1　Misunderstanding mentoring

Problems can occur if there is a lack of awareness of the process itself, and what it is designed to achieve. This is the responsibility of the organization, and should be the subject of careful consideration at the outset. If a consultant is used to advise on the introduction of mentoring, the organization will come under considerable scrutiny for this aspect of the process. Attention to communication is necessary for all players to understand that the process is critical to later success.

5.8.2　Lack of preparation

Lack of training and preparation can jeopardize what would otherwise be a successful relationship. Both mentor and protégé should be able to prepare for the scheme, but both should be able to admit to areas which need particular development. The SWOT analysis which the protégé is encouraged to carry out could be equally appropriate for the mentor in order to ascertain their training needs for this role. Organizations should not anticipate that successful managers will be equally successful mentors purely on the basis of their existing experience. The role of mentor is special, and therefore needs particular attention. Training is one aspect, support is another and there will be benefit from monitoring mentors as well as the success in meeting the objectives of the protégé.

Training cannot accommodate all possible eventualities. It can happen that a mentoring relationship can flounder when the rules are inadvertently broken. The introduction of subjects which appear innocuous can trigger unanticipated outcomes for which neither mentor nor protégé are prepared. The exclusion of discussion of personal areas in the contract can assist this, but not prevent it altogether.

5.8.3 Selection processes

These can be arbitrary. Resentment can occur in employees who are not being mentored due to there being insufficient mentors to 'go round'. This can be exacerbated if those who are protégés go on to be successful in terms of promotion. Careful attention to the selection criteria, in the same way as recruitment procedures are usually monitored, will eliminate criticism of this type.

5.8.4 Cross-gender mentoring

This can pose a problem. Library organizations may still not be able to provide female mentors for new female employees, although there may be an improvement from the situation in 1988, when only 2% of women were in the salary bracket which would identify them as in senior positions. The figure, taken from The Library Association survey of 1992[9] indicates a rise of 6% and this will undoubtedly increase. Gender can be a problem for women who are mentored by men. The absence of the role model as a criterion in the relationship, or the behavioural problems associated with cross-gender mentoring, are examined in Maack and Passett[10] and Kram.[11]

5.8.5 Expectations and demands

The most common cause quoted in the literature for failure, is that of mismatch of personality. However, as the mentoring relationship is a relationship, there may well be some movement in the attitudes of both mentor and protégé due to the changing circumstances of both parties. As the protégé matures and increases his/her confidence, he/she will exhibit tendencies towards independence to which the mentor must react. This can be a testing time for the mentor. Changes in the responsibilities of the mentor can bring about similar changes in time and availability which make them appear more distant and less involved. Acknowledging these changes as they occur, and signalling the potential danger, may be all that can be done without withdrawing from the relationship altogether. If a break is required, the protégé can feel abandoned and have to face starting again. The essential ingredient in the mentoring relationship is honesty. Being honest will not solve the problems, but will enable the preparation for change to be addressed more openly.

5.8.6 Summary

David Clutterbuck[4] quotes two surveys in his assessment of 'problems of the mentoring relationship'. One survey carried out in 1986[12] (published 1990) shows that the difficulties in mentoring result from:

- inadequate definition of the roles

- level of commitment
- lack of continuity from training programme to post-training career
- resentment from the line manager of the protégé

The Industrial Society survey of 1989[6] (published 1990) gave the following as the most usual reasons for failure of mentoring arrangements:

- inadequate feedback
- time constraints on mentors
- mis-matches between mentors and protégés
- frequent moves of site, resulting in changes of mentor for a protégé

5.9 Mini case-study: Miami-Dade faculty mentor program

The Miami-Dade Community College, America's largest multi-campus community college, created a teaching/learning project to improve student satisfaction. One of the strands identified in a résumé of the initiative,[13] and the resulting programme for improvement was 'faculty excellence'. Qualities and characteristics were identified for excellent teaching and non-teaching faculty, and these were integrated and developed into recommended procedures for recruitment, selection and integration of new faculty into the college. A new induction programme developed from a survey of the previous new faculty, and mentoring was seen to be beneficial in the integration process.

In the Miami-Dade faculty mentor program (see Badley[13]) mentors are expected to:

- Review course objectives and departmental information on courses.
- Review teaching strategies for specific units.
- Invite new faculty members to sit in on student advisement (sic) sessions (tutorials).
- Provide orientation to surroundings (on and off campus, based on responsibilites).
- Provide 'helpful hints' to the new teacher to help make daily activities run smoothly.
- Help new faculty to anticipate problem areas.
- Have lunch with new faculty members.
- Be a comprehensive resource on curriculum planning, presentations, class management, student motivation and student evaluation.
- Accompany new faculty member to faculty senate meeting.
- Schedule meeting with new faculty member on weekly basis (1 hour).
- Contact faculty in department to encourage them to invite new faculty member to sit in on their classes.
- Complete training on classroom observation, and be available to sit in on new faculty member's classes and give feedback to faculty member (focus on content, teaching style and strategies).
- Personally introduce the new faculty member to all other department members and to key resource/service personnel on campus.
- Provide advice, direction and encouragement.
- Attend a reception for new faculty and introduce new faculty member to those attending.
- Look for all opportunities to make the new faculty member feel welcome.

The first desirable quality looked for in a mentor was the willingness to become one, and the list of expectations appears daunting. It is easy to interpret the above list for educational organizations, and it provides a good overall view of the type of activity which mentors can legitimately undertake on behalf of their protégés. Others included 'personal warmth' and 'empathy', as well as the previously mentioned sense of humour and an ability to listen.

A training programme was devised, and the mentors were provided with a fee for this work. Evaluation was through feedback from the new faculty and from mentors themselves. The initiative was generally thought to be a positive one.

References

1 Handy, C., *The age of unreason*, London, Arrow 1990.
2 Parry, J., *Induction*, London, Library Association Publishing Limited, 1993.
3 Williamson, M., *Training needs analysis*, London, Library Association Publishing Limited, 1993.
4 Clutterbuck, D., *Everyone needs a mentor*, (2nd edn.), London, IPM, 1991.
5 Hamilton, R., *Mentoring*, London, The Industrial Society, 1993.
6 The Industrial Society and the ITEM Group, *The line manager's role in developing talent*, London, The Industrial Society, 1990.
7 The Industrial Society, *Training report no 4*, London, The Industrial Society, 1992.
8 Caldwell, B. J. and Carter, E. M. A., *Return of the mentor*, London, Falmer Press, 1993.
9 The Library Association, *Equal opportunities in the library profession*, London, The Library Association, 1992.
10 Maack, M. N. and Passett, J., *Aspirations and mentoring in an academic environment; women faculty in library and information science*, London, Greenwood Press, 1994.
11 Kram, K. *Mentoring at work: developmental relationships in organisational life*, Glenview Illinois, Scott Foresman and Co., 1985.
12 PA Consulting Group, *Management development and mentoring: an international study*, London, PA Consulting Group, 1990.
13 Badley, G. 'Institutional values and teaching quality', in Barnett, R. (ed.), *Learning to effect*, Buckingham, The Society for Research into Higher Education and The Open University, 1992.

6 Variations of mentoring

6.1 Informal mentoring

If an organization has not introduced mentoring, it is still possible to find someone to advise in many work-related situations. People who acquire the appropriate skills of coaching and counselling may become external mentors to those in different types of organization. These relationships may be between members of the same profession (and this is frequent in librarianship), or between a mentor who has achieved a position which is parallel to that to which the protégé aspires. As this is a matter of selection and choice between individuals not in any way connected, this is referred to as informal mentoring.

Although the main aim of this guide is to indicate how formal mentoring schemes can be established, there are many readers who will wish to develop mentoring for other reasons. They may have been asked to be a mentor, or they may wish to seek a mentor. They may feel that understanding mentoring will enable them to undertake other managerial roles more successfully. It may be that they wish to establish in their own minds a picture of mentoring, and the benefits which accrue from it. Gill Burrington[1] emphasizes the need for informal mentors to do their work properly. The use of the Henley Distance Learning mentoring kit (see Appendix C) may assist this process.

6.1.1 The advantages

Many of the individuals in *Equally good* by Gill Burrington[1] attribute their success to mentoring, or to the presence of mentors at critical stages of their career development. In all cases, it was the permissive nature of the mentors which had the greatest impact. The ability to make mistakes, and to learn from them, is sometimes overlooked in the quest for success.

A management theory which is focused on planning for success may lead individuals to believe that failure is unacceptable and the initiative must always be 'right first time'. While this search for perfection is admirable, it is also unrealistic. An informal mentor will certainly encourage the protégé to find options amongst solutions but, important though work is, this wise adviser will also provide a clear and essential perspective on the balance between work, and the rest of the protégé's life, without the overriding need to meet an organization's objectives in doing so.

There are critical times when an informal mentor can assist, for example if a protégé is contemplating a career move or considering the wisdom of remaining with a particular organization. Once a career move has been achieved, it can take some time before an individual can identify a person with whom a mentoring relationship is possible. It is at these times that the availability of someone to talk through 'areas of the unknown' is critical to the absorption of the new culture and the strange surroundings.

6.1.2 The disadvantages

There are arguments against the proliferation of informal mentoring within organizations, on the grounds that it is more easily obtained by those assertive and confident individuals who are able to attract the attention of senior members of staff. This group will probably succeed through their own ambition and talent, without the 'patronage' of these senior people. David Clutterbuck[2] claims that informal mentoring gives such individuals unfair advantage over those who fail to make the right connections with those in high positions. Formal mentoring eliminates élitism, providing an egalitarian system of ensuring the development of all who are qualified to succeed within an organization.

Informal mentoring can be more difficult to sustain. The mentor and protégé may live at some distance from each other and thus the geography may not facilitate the necessary high degree of contact during the early stages. Where there is limited similarity between the work areas of the mentor and protégé, it can also be difficult to deal with problems connected with the politics of the organization.

6.2 Mentors and professional development

The mentor should encourage participation in the profession, either through a professional body such as The Library Association or Institute of Information Scientists, or by contributions to the literature in the chosen area. The Institute of Personnel Management (IPM) is introducing a profession-wide mentoring scheme for new members. The publishing industry has already established mentoring as a career development tool for women.

6.3 Master mentors

This is a term used by David Clutterbuck[3] when talking about the need for mentors to cascade their acquired mentoring knowledge on to other potential mentors. Many managers will acquire the skills required for successful mentoring, but the process of bringing them together into the mentoring process will need support in training (see section 5.8.2). The mentors, once established, can then take responsibility for the preparation of other mentors within the organization. This process will assist the organization to develop sufficient mentors to meet their requirements.

6.4 Mentoring for open or distance learning

Open and distance learning are attractive methods of taking further courses which help people to gain additional qualifications. Most often, this type of study is followed by those whose time or other commitments do not allow study through the more usual full-time, part-time or day-release modes.

The Northern Training Group (NTG), in association with the Scottish Council for Education Technology, (SCET) (see Appendix C) has produced open learning materials to meet the particular needs of public library staff. These 'interactive' materials enable 'students' to establish their own pace as they work through a specially designed learning package, as for example in financial management.

Advice is provided about how to avoid the isolation which open or distance learners may experience, and one of the options suggested is to ask a mentor to help with the learning process. Although the role of the line manager is suggested for specific information about the particular task or to create learning opportunities, friends or colleagues are also possible options.

In these cases mentors will need to familiarize themselves with the work to be done, the objectives of the course and, most importantly, to understand the learning process involved in this type of learning. At all times the learner must be in control of the pace of work, and the final decisions about any of the learning objectives or presentations are entirely his/hers. In these cases, the protégé (learner) must establish what it is he/she requires from his/her mentor, and the mentor must adapt to the role by offering the type of support required. The NTG/SCET packs include a mentor's guide, as well as a learner's guide, but no other documentation.

A learning contract is suggested by the NTG and SCET which sets out the learner's intentions and how they intend to fulfil them along with target dates. The mentor may at this stage specify the amount of time, and the type of support necessary to define their commitment to the arrangement. Progress can be monitored by the student through the use of the progress charts which accompany the packs, or by the use of a checklist of activities. The learning log or diary approach is also suggested as a way of 'keeping on track'.

6.5   Mentoring for work-based learning

An interesting initiative which Leeds Metropolitan University began in 1992 focuses on the role of the workplace mentor in the context of work-based learning (Leeds Metropolitan University, 1993). An investigation, funded by the Department of Employment, set out to identify the role of the mentor in specific work-based degree courses.

An initiative from Clwyd Library Service has established a role for librarians in the use of open learning materials which are retained within the local public libraries. 'Supporting learner partnerships' was a project which employed new modes and channels of learner support in initial teacher education. It was funded by the National Council for Educational Technology (NCET), and supported by the School of Education, University of Wales, Bangor; Clwyd Library Service; and Gwynedd Local Education Authority Education Resources Centre. Librarians were trained as mentors for those participating in the open learning for the postgraduate certificate in education (PGCE) courses who were on school placements where available resources were insufficient to meet their learning needs.

One of the professions to use mentoring as an essential part of the learning process is teaching. A full description of the process is given in *The school mentor handbook* by Hagger.[4] However there have been considerable changes in the qualification route for teachers as a result of government decisions. Mentoring has become a requirement for those trained teachers who are supervising trainee teachers on placement in schools. It has been suggested that the involuntary nature of this type of mentoring does not provide for a full assessment of the needs of organization, mentor and protégé that has been suggested earlier in this text.

6.6   Summary

Apart from the organization-based mentoring, there are other applications which individuals may wish to explore. The requirements for a mentor remain the same as those outlined in Chapter 4. The challenge of meeting the requirements to be a successful mentor needs the same attention to the process, the same development of the skills and the same understanding of the commitment, irrespective of the actual 'type' of mentoring.

References

1 Burrington, G., *Equally good*, London, Association of Assistant Librarians, 1993.
2 Clutterbuck, D., 'Blooming managers', *Management training*, **February**, 1994, 17–19.
3 Clutterbuck, D., *Everyone needs a mentor*, (2nd edn.), London, IPM, 1991.
4 Hagger, H, Burn, K, and McIntyre, D., *The school mentor handbook*, London, Kogan Page, 1993.

Conclusion

7.1   What is mentoring?

Mentoring defies a single definition. Its value is in the ways in which organizations and individuals use the process for improvement and growth. There is a considerable literature focused on practice in the United Kingdom as well as North America. University research in Britain, together with the work carried out by the European Mentoring Centre, ensures a growing body of work to complement the practice of mentoring within organizations.

7.2   Why should mentoring be introduced?

One survey by The Industrial Society[1] provides quantitative and qualitative data to support the introduction of an effective mentoring operation. Descriptions of mentoring systems from other organizations offer models of good employment practice, which may lead other organizations towards the 'learning organizations', as defined by Handy,[2] Pedler,[3] and Senge.[4] This is currently seen as positive development for employees, and for their employing organizations.

7.3   When should mentoring be used?

Mentoring can be used at various times within a career, and should be seen as a way of moving forward from one position to another, as a tool for professional development and as a check on the extremes of one's own vision of the future. There will be a time when the experiences of one's own mentoring may lead to a decision to become a mentor for another, thus cascading the practice of mentoring.

7.4   What can be gained from mentoring?

Each protégé should know what it is they want from mentoring. It is only right that the protégé is as prepared for the experience as the mentor, by reading about mentoring, understanding his/her own needs and realizing the commitment which he/she is making to his/her own career. Seeing the mentoring scheme as a contract should give some indication of the seriousness with which the process should be regarded. It is a two-way process, and the benefits to be gained by having advice and experience provided by a senior person should be seen as a privileged opportunity for career and personal growth.

7.5   The skills required for mentoring

For those considering mentoring, the important areas to address are the skills and the qualities required to be a good mentor. There is some value in undertaking specific skills training, although many mentors or potential mentors will have acquired the skills via other routes. Courses which bring together skills for mentoring provide an extra dimension and illustrate ways in which various skills can be combined to build up a profile of a mentor.

7.6 Selecting a formal mentoring scheme

Formal mentoring schemes will vary depending upon the company, organization or academic institution. It is important that any organization establishing a formal mentoring scheme should take time to provide a scheme which most fits the organization. This role should not be left to chance if all involved - mentors, protégés, line managers and training officers - are to understand the purpose of the scheme.

7.7 Drawing up a mentoring training outline

It will be necessary to draw up a planning schedule with appropriate training checklists, skills requirements, documentation and evaluation processes, all integrated into the design of the mentoring training outline. Other Library Training Guides will be helpful in all these processes. There are many schemes to be found in a variety of different organizations. In order to choose the right one, it may be necessary to take professional advice from one of the organizations listed in Appendix B. The wrong sort of mentoring scheme can be disastrous for all concerned, wasting time and financial resources as well as providing negative experiences for those involved.

7.8 What can go wrong?

Mentoring can go wrong for a variety of reasons; some of the literature referred to has given the main reasons for failure. This is summarized by David Cluttebuck[5] in *Everyone needs a mentor*. Judicious use of the experience of personnel professionals may save the mentoring relationship which is showing signs of stress or failure. The honesty and integrity of the mentor can be the way to resolve the situation with dignity.

7.9 Summary

Mentoring can be one of the most positive experiences of one's career, and it has many other applications too. The Library Association has now established the Continuing Professional Development Framework. The complementary process of providing oneself with a mentor is one positive way of ensuring successful career planning and development.

References

1 Gibb, S. and Megginson, D., 'Inside corporate mentoring schemes: a new agenda of concerns', *Personnel review*, **22** (1), 1993, 40–54.
2 Handy, C., *The age of unreason*, London, Arrow, 1990.
3 Pedler, M., Burgoyne, J. and Boydell, T., *The learning company*, London, McGraw-Hill, 1991.
4 Senge, P.M., *The fifth discipline: the art and practice of the learning organisation*, New York, Doubleday Currency, 1990.
5 Clutterbuck, D., *Everyone needs a mentor* (2nd edn.), London, IPM, 1991.

Appendix A
Bibliography

Badley, G. 'Institutional values and teaching quality', in Barnett, R. (ed.), *Learning to effect*, Buckingham, The Society for Research into Higher Education and The Open University, 1992.

Burke, M. E., 'Career development report: one perspective', *Personnel, training and education*, **9** (3), 1992, 76–7.

Burrington, G., *Equally good*, London, Association of Assistant Librarians, 1993.

Burrington, G., 'Mentors – a source of skill, strength and enthusiasm', *Library Association record*, **95** (4), 1993, 226–7.

Caldwell, B. J. and Carter, E. M. A., *Return of the mentor*, London, Falmer Press, 1993.

Carter, S., 'The development, implementation and evaluation of a mentoring scheme', *Industrial and commercial training*, **7**, July, 1994.

Caulkin, S., 'Let my people profit', *Observer business section*, 6 March, 1994, 8.

Charlton, S., 'Networking for guerrillas', *The bookseller*, 21 August, 1992, 468–70.

Clutterbuck, D., 'Blooming managers', *Management training*, February, 1994, 17–19.

Clutterbuck, D., *Everyone needs a mentor*, (2nd edn.), London, IPM, 1991.

Clutterbuck, D., *Mentoring*, Henley on Thames, Henley Distance Learning Ltd., 1992.

Darling, L. A. W., 'The mentoring discovery process: helping people manage their mentoring', *Mentoring international*, **3** (2), 1989, 12–16.

Dodgson, J., 'Do women in education need mentors?', *Education Canada*, Spring, 1986, 29.

Edwards, S., 'The IPM's new flexible route to learning', *Personnel management*, December, 1992, 38–41.

Falconer, H., 'Bowing to experience', *Personnel today*, 7–20 April, 1992, 25–8.

Ferriero, D.S., 'ARL directors as protégés and mentors, *Journal of academic librarianship*, **7** (6), 1982, 358–65.

Gardiner, J., Gielnik, C. and Brough, L., *Women's training, career and development opportunities*, London, The Industrial Society. 1993.

Gibb, S. and Megginson, D., 'Inside corporate mentoring schemes: a new agenda of concerns', *Personnel review*, **22** (1), 1993, 40–54.

Hagger, H., Burn, K., and McIntyre, D., *The school mentor handbook*, London, Kogan Page, 1993.

Hamilton, R., *Mentoring*, London, The Industrial Society, 1993.

Handy, C., *The age of unreason*, London, Arrow, 1990.

Harris, R. M., 'The mentoring trap', *Library journal*, **118** (17), 1993, 37–9.

Head, F. and Gray, M. M., 'The legacy of Mentor: insights into western history, literature and the media', *International journal of mentoring*, **2** (2), 1988, 26–33.

Heirs, B. and Farrell, P., *The professional decision-thinker*, London, Grafton, 1989.

Honey, P. and Mumford, A., *The manual of learning opportunities*, London, 1989.

Hunt, D. M. and Michael, C., 'Mentorship: a career training and development tool', *Journal of library administration*, 1984, 77–95.

The Industrial Society and the ITEM Group, *The line manager's role in developing talent. Coaching, mentoring, counselling*, London, The Industrial Society, 1990.

The Industrial Society, *Training Report No. 4*, London, The Industrial Society, 1992.

Institution of Industrial Managers, *Qualifications for operations and industrial managers. Programme and regulations*, The Leader Series, Corby, Institution of Industrial Managers, 1992.

Jackson, C., 'Mentoring: choices for individuals and organisations', *The international journal of career management*, **5** (1), 1993, 10–16.

Kelly, M., Beck, T. and Thomas, J., 'More than a supporting act', *Times educational supplement*, 8 November, 1991, 17.

Kolb, D., *Experiential learning*, New York, Prentice Hall, 1984.

Kolb, D. and Fry, R., 'Towards an applied theory of experiential learning', in Cooper, C. L. (ed.), *Theories of group process*, Chichester, Wiley, 1975.

Kram, K., *Mentoring at work: developmental relationships in organisational life*, Glenview, Illinois, Scott Foresman and Co., 1985.

Leeds Metropolitan University, *Mentoring: the 'working for a degree' project*, Leeds, 1993 (Library Training Guide).

Levinson, D. J., Darrow, C. N., Klein, E. B., Levinson, M. H. and McKee, B., *The seasons of a man's life*, New York, A. A. Knopf Inc., 1978.

Levy, P., *Interpersonal skills*, London, Library Association Publishing Limited, 1993 (Library Training Guide).

The Library Association, *Equal opportunities in the library profession*, London, The Library Association, 1992.

Maack, M. N. and Passett, J., *Aspirations and mentoring in an academic environment; women faculty in library and information science*, London, Greenwood Press, 1994.

Morris, B., *Training and development for women*, London, Library Association Publishing Limited, 1993 (Library Training Guide).

Mumford, A., *Developing directors: the learning process*, London, Manpower Services Commission, 1987.

Newman, G. C., Dibartolo, A. and Hill, L., 'Fostering professional growth in academic libraries: a case study for the 1990s', *Library administration and management*, Winter, 1991, 41–4.

Northern Training Group and Scottish Council for Education Technology, *Financial management for librarians: mentor's guide*, Newcastle NTG/SCET, 1994.

OTSU Ltd, 'Mentoring in a flexible training system', *Open learning today*, October 1992, 8, March 1993, 5, May 1993, 10–11, July 1993, 3.

PA Consulting Group, *Management development and mentoring: an international study*, London, PA Consulting Group, 1990.

Palmer, T., 'Mentoring: what's in it for mentors?', *Employment digest: Personnel in practice*, **376**, 18 April, 1994, 1–3.

Parry, J., *Induction*, London, Library Association Publishing Limited, 1993 (Library Training Guide).

Parsloe, E., *Coaching, mentoring and assessing: a practical guide to developing competence*, London, Kogan Page, 1992.

Peach, L., 'Planning careers', *Personnel today*, 23 November, 1993, 15.

Pedler, M., Burgoyne, J. and Boydell, T., *The learning company*, London, McGraw-Hill, 1991.

Phillips-Jones, L., *Mentors and protégés*, New York, Arbor House, 1982.

Quinn, J., 'Me and my mentor', *Library journal*, **116** (13), 1991, 53.

Roberts, D. L., 'Mentoring in the academic library', *College and research library news*, February, 1986, 117–19.

Senge, P.M., *The fifth discipline: the art and practice of the learning organisation*, New York, Doubleday Currency, 1990.

Shea, G. F., *Mentoring*, London, Kogan Page, 1992.

Snow, M., 'On my mind – librarian as mentor,' *Journal of academic librarianship*, **16** (3), 1990, 163–4.

Taylor, S., 'Managing a learning environment', *Personnel management*, October, 1992, 54–7.

Trask, M. and Wood, J., *Career planning and assessment for librarians*, Lindfield, N.S.W., College of Advanced Education, 1984.

Wilkin, M., *Mentoring in schools*, London, Kogan Page, 1992.

Williamson, M., *Training needs analysis*, London, Library Association Publishing Limited, 1993 (Library Training Guide).

Zey, M., *The mentor connection*, Homewood, Ill., Dow Jones-Irwin, 1984.

Zey, M., 'Mentoring programmes: making the right moves', *Personnel journal*, **64** (2), 1985, 53–7.

Appendix B
Examples of organizations using mentoring

The following are examples of firms or other organizations which have recognized the value of mentoring and have introduced it as a formal system.

Ashridge Management College
Berkampsted, Herts HP4 1NS. Viki Holton: Senior Researcher.
Tel: 0442 843491

Ashridge are management consultants who have worked with a variety of firms in the UK, USA and Europe. They advised Staffordshire University in the setting up of their mentoring for women scheme (op. cit.) in 1992.

The Ashridge process includes a considerable investigation of the organization and its reasons for introducing mentoring. It offers 'learning points', in order to achieve the aims and objectives of the organization.

ICL Staff Learning
ICL Beaumont, Old Windsor, SL4 2JP

Despite ICL having a history of self-managed learning, they acknowledge that it is not possible to introduce mentoring throughout the organization. They have introduced mentoring for new, graduate entrants to the organization. Their director of human resources management, Andrew Mayo, claims that the output of people is limited unless there is investment in their capacity; in the same way as any production company will invest in plant, so they should consider investment in people. Mayo acknowledges the essential of being a 'learning organization' and describes ICL Staff Learning as 'part of the corporate glue', this was described in an interview with Simon Caulkin in *The Observer* newspaper business section of 6 March 1994 (p8).

ICL saw the problem of a skills shortage being answered by systematic training. Training did not necessarily mean successful learning. Self-development, if encouraged alongside training, was seen to enhance the process.

ICL required that this was in some way 'business related' and mentors were involved, in order to ensure that there was a direct link between the development plans of individuals and organizational aims and objectives, to open doors and provide ideas for their protégés, as well as offering a helicopter view of the organization.

The mentoring scheme was launched at a senior development team meeting and the Henley mentoring kit was used to provide the documentation. Volunteer mentors were enlisted and their CV's collected, and a list provided from which protégés chose.

Some criticism arose, including the feeling that this prescriptive method of ensuring the organizational objectives were being achieved, was at odds with the principles of the self-managed learning programme it was established to complement. There are now options for all following the self-managed learning programme: either self-selection of a mentor, no mentor at all, or assistance through one of the Learning Consultants which ICL employ.

Individuals can establish their own development needs, and mentoring has been of two kinds: the 'opening doors' senior-level view and the confidence development tool, where the coaching/counselling roles are the dominant ones played by the mentor. ICL have accepted that there are three relevant areas of development where mentoring can assist: current job development, career development, or learning about learning.

There continues to be positive feedback and ICL are convinced that mentoring is an essential part of their self-managed learning programme. Future initiatives for ICL include a day where mentors come together and share and compare their experiences.

Institute of Manpower Studies

Mantell Building, University of Sussex, Falmer, Brighton BN1 9RF
Tel: 0273 686751

Courses: Training administrator, Janet Mortimer. Tel: 0273 678181
Mentoring specialist, Charles Jackson

The Institute provides a range of services related to human resource management. The 'Training calendar' offers courses which are open to all. In addition, the Institute carries out research and consultancy work for employers, employee bodies and professional bodies. There is particular emphasis on career planning and development. The Institute develops courses for individual organizations if required.

Mentoring is included in one of the IMS Forum Series courses, *Career planning: promoting 'self-development' for individuals.*

The Institute of Management

Management House, Cottingham Road, Corby, Northamptonshire NN17 1TT. Tel: 0536 204222

Mentoring specialist: Steve Carter
Head of Management Development

The Institute provides members with a comprehensive management information service offered by the Management Information Centre. The enquiry service, reading lists for managers (mentoring is included in 'Coaching and counselling), tailored searches, as well as book loans, photocopies and on-line searches, can be supplemented by specialized research undertaken by MIC's Information Researchers.

The Institute's mentoring expert is Steve Carter, who is the author of an article on mentoring and who has contributed to the IM's book on mentoring which is planned for future publication.

The European Mentoring Centre

Burnham House, High Street, Burnham, Buckinghamshire SL1 7JZ
Tel: 0628 604882

An innovative development by one of Britain's best-known authors and experts on mentoring, David Clutterbuck, and associates David Megginson, Alan Mumford and Bernard Wynne.

The centre offers corporate membership, and a range of information services and other activities for those who wish to establish and operate formal mentoring programmes, or to explore the relevance of mentoring for their organization.

The Centre has four main activities: research and development into best practice, maintenance of a mentoring database, training of mentors and protégés, and assistance in establishing and operating formal mentoring programmes.

Institute of Training & Development
ITD Training Limited, Marlow House, Institute Road, Marlow, Buckinghamshire SL7 1BN. Tel: 0628 8901213

Contact Jo Dickie

ITD/HRD current planning for mentoring includes an ambitious programme to host an international mentoring event, in conjunction with the European Mentoring Centre, and a course, 'Mentoring to improve performance'.

ITD/HRD also produce a 'Toolkit for the learning organization'. This toolkit assists those organizations wishing to develop this approach by presenting ideas, processes exercises in conjunction with an Introductory Workshop, and provides membership of the 'Learning organization toolkit user group'.

Women into Information Technology
The WIT Foundation, Concept 2000, 250 Farnborough Road, Farnborough Hampshire GU14 7LU. Tel: 0252 528329

The Women into Information Technology Foundation Limited (WIT) offers institutional and individual membership to those wishing to promote roles for women in an increasingly IT-rich environment. The organization recognizes mentoring as a significant tool for women's development, and have now run two courses for women and mentoring. WIT is a good example of an organization which sees the value of applying a particular human resource development to a specific group of individuals.

Roffey Park Management Institute
Horsham, West Sussex RH12 4TD. Tel: 0293 851644

Contact Joanna Howard

Roffey Park Management Institute offer a range of courses to improve management performance. In their advice to those who wish to explore mentoring, they address the needs for the organization, the senior manager and those who are to benefit from mentoring. They acknowledge the fact that many of those enrolling for MBA courses are already working in management positions, and thus they bring together the mentoring for individuals on courses with the requirement for future (and existing) managers to mentor.

Henley Distance Learning
Craigmore House, Remenham Hill, Henley-on-Thames, OXON RG9 3EP
Tel: 0491 571552. Fax: 0491 579843

Henley Distance Learning offers a variety of courses. Mentoring is one of several development methods which are available within the 'Diploma in

Management and Organisation Development' course. Henley Distance Learning recommend that their courses in Management and Organization Development follow a pattern of programmed implementation including mentor support. This may be from one person within the organization, possibly a training officer, personnel manager or line manager or someone especially chosen. Whichever alternative is chosen, the functions to be provided are counselling, motivating, tutoring and active provision of experiential learning opportunities. The objective is to provide effective support for the learner and to help them transfer their learning to work.

Institute of Personnel Management
IPM House, Camp Road, Wimbledon, London SW19 4UX. Tel: 081 946 9100

Membership Development Manager, Christine Williams

The IPM South West London Branch set up a mentoring system on a pilot basis, to provide professional support for newly qualified professionals, who were in the early stages of their personnel career.

A pilot mentoring scheme for personnel professionals was introduced after six months of research, carried out by a 'Mentoring steering committee'. All training was provided by the IPM Branch, free of charge. It is a fairly informal scheme, but there is considerable emphasis placed on monitoring the development and success of future applications in other branches of the IPM.

The research included a feasibility study, the identification of participants (mentors and protégés), a survey on potential participation, an examination of the required timescale for implementation and a costing.

Planning required the commitment of all members of the branch ('from top to bottom'), the establishment of guidelines for the programme, a set of 'eligibility criteria' and a launch.

Implementation required people being invited to join the scheme, the selection and training of mentors and protégés, establishing matching criteria for the matching process and setting up effective co-ordination and administration.

Monitoring and evaluation, critical to the continued success of the scheme, involves on-going monitoring, measuring the achievement of the objectives, determining the strengths and weaknesses and attempting to analyse the success of the scheme.

The Industrial Society
48 Bryanston Square, London W1H 7LN. Tel: 071 262 2401

Mentoring expert: Jenny Sweeney, Senior Consultant

The Industrial Society has an established reputation in the provision of objective advice, consultancy and research on a range of employment-related and human resource development issues. The two surveys on mentoring in United Kingdom businesses, which The Industrial Society have already carried out, provide a basis for a future trend analysis.

The Industrial Society has also commissioned and published a book on mentoring, written by Reg Hamilton and published in 1993.

Appendix C
Examples of programmes in use by firms or other organizations when training for mentoring

1   Mentoring for protégés: The BBC
2   Organizational mentoring: The European Mentoring Centre
3   A programme for all parties engaged in organization-wide mentoring: Henley Distance Learning
4   Training programmes for librarians: The Burrington Partnership
5   Open learning materials for library staff: NTG & SCET
6   Mentoring to improve performance:ITD Training Ltd
7   Professional development for women: Women into Information Technology
8   Mentoring for senior managers: Roffey Park Management Institute

| Example 1 | Mentoring for protégés: The BBC |

This is an example of a training programme specifically designed for those who wished to be mentored. It was developed by the BBC's Staff Development Department, Corporate Management Development Division.

The BBC introduced mentoring in 1990. The documentation reproduced here is that provided for anyone wishing to select a mentor.

Staff Development Department

MENTORING

The Mentoring Process

Mentoring is a process which involves a relationship between a more senior and a more junior employee (usually not boss/subordinate). Through this the more junior employee is helped to develop both professionally and personally.

Whilst some people are happiest operating in groups for their support, others prefer one to one relationships. If you're one of the latter, you might like to work with a mentor.

What Do You Want From A Mentor?

The first step in finding a mentor is to think carefully about what you want from a mentoring relationship. Until you've worked this out, you won't know what kind of person to choose.

What you want from a mentor will depend upon your needs. It may be, for example, that you anticipate your greatest difficulty will be in maintaining your motivation during your job search. In this case, you might want a Mentor who is full of enthusiasm and plans their work well.

To help you focus your thoughts, the following are some of the roles a mentor could offer you.

Possible Roles of a Mentor

- a tutor eg offering insight into the managerial process

- a source of advice eg about the BBC

- a sounding board eg someone to bat ideas around with

- a coach eg on matters to do with your own individual style and inter-personal skills

- a confidante - someone with whom to talk through problems on a confidential basis

- a guide eg through BBC politics and systems

Staff Development Department
CORPORATE MANAGEMENT DEVELOPMENT DIVISION

Example 1 continued

- a route to others ie giving you access to the Mentor's network

- a role model

- a champion eg letting others know of your value to the
organisation

- a friend.

This list is not exhaustive. Each mentoring relationship is
unique and depends upon the two individuals involved so the range
of roles is extensive.

Choosing a Mentor

Having decided what you want from a mentor and what sort of roles
you want them to provide for you, you now need to think about the
type of person who best fits your needs. Your choice of person
may depend on some of these factors:-

1   Do your want them to have similar or contrasting work
    experience to you or a mixture: What is their work
    experience? At what stage is their career?

2   Do you want to work with someone who is senior in the
    organisation, possibly with influence, clout, inside
    knowledge, a "good" reputation, or would you prefer someone
    nearer to your own level who might more easily identify
    with your problems?

3   Is it important that they have good inter-personal skills
    and if so which eg empathy, a good listener and
    communicator.

4   Do you need ready access to them? How busy are they and
    are they likely to make time for you?

5   How responsive are they and can they be flexible for your
    individual needs?

6   Do you want someone with a wide and/or deep knowledge of
    the BBC and current issues?

7   Is it important your mentor is familiar with theories and
    developments outside the BBC?

8   Do you want a mentor with a contrasting or similar style?

9   Does this person have a track record of bringing on people?

10 Are there particular skills you would want them to have
    and/or a wide range?

11 Is it important that you can tap into their network of
    contacts?

12 Do you want to work with someone of your own gender?

Example 1 continued

13 What is the likelihood that they will respond positively to your request to become your mentor?

A Word of Caution

Before you approach someone to become your mentor, bear in mind that mentoring is not an easy option. You may like to consider:-

a Mentoring requires a lot of commitment from both you an the mentor in terms of:

time - you will need to find time in your diary for regular sessions with your mentor

emotional resources - your mentor may confront you with issues you'd rather brush under the carpet!

sustained effort - the more you work at it, the more the relationship will have value for you.

b How will you feel if the person you approach declines your request to become a mentor?

c What is your boss likely to think about the mentoring relationship? Will they feel threatened?

d What if the mentoring relationship doesn't work out?

Selling Mentoring To A Potential Mentor

When you approach your chosen person, you may need to market the idea of mentoring to them, so it is useful to have some thoughts about how the relationship could help them. For example, they might achieve:-

1 Improved job satisfaction

- this could be a challenging and interesting opportunity for them

- they may feel pride in the way they are helping you to develop

2 Peer recognition

- for having been selected to be a mentor

- for having you as their protege

3 Career advancement

through - developing ideas with you
- getting work done by you
- enhancing their reputation as someone who develops people.

Example 1   continued

Your First Meeting

Your first meeting with your mentor is going to be an opportunity for you to set the ground rules of the relationship. It will be important for each of you to know what to expect and how you'll operate so neither are disappointed and each knows where they stand. You may want a checklist for discussion which could include:-

1   What are our expectations of this relationship?

   - what roles do each of us expect to take on and have shown to us?

   - how much is each prepared to do? eg is your mentor prepared to share contacts; are you prepared to take risks.

'2   How do we want to manage our meetings?

   - How frequent

   - How long

   - Over what period

   - Venue

   - Structure

3   How does this relationship affect your relationship with your line manager?

Thereafter

You and your mentor will develop your own way of working together. You may decide to continue the relationship if it works well. It could be the most significant step in your career. Research amongst senior managers in the BBC has shown that the most significant factor in the career advancement of 2/3 of the sample was the existence of a mentor who took an interest in their development.

SN
06.12.90

AS UPDATE
30.05.91

Example 2   **Organizational mentoring: The European Mentoring Centre:**

The Mentor Development Workshop is offered by The European Mentoring Centre for those organizations wishing to introduce mentoring. It would be adapted to the particular organization and elements could be tailored to suit the particular objectives agreed with an organization's managers.

Mentor Development Workshop
Workshop designed by David Clutterbuck, for The European Mentoring Centre.

```
MENTOR DEVELOPMENT WORKSHOP

9:00am
Introduction

A background to mentoring      20 mins
Presentation by David Clutterbuck on the origins and dimensions
of mentoring

Brief discussion: how many of you have had a mentor?   15 mins

Line managers' responsibility for developing the talent of other
people in the organisation.   20 mins
Discussion of the concepts.
Syndicate exercise.   To what extent do managers in our
organisation take this responsibility? How will the cultural and
structural changes we expect impact on these responsibilities?

The environment for learning  40 mins
Syndicate discussion of how managers learn and communicate.  How
will this affect relationships between mentors and mentees?

What do we expect to achieve from the relationship?    40 mins
- for the protege?
- for the organisation?
- for the mentors?
Syndicate sessions

What makes a good mentor?      30 mins
Exercises and discussion to establish what makes a good mentor
in this company.
(Start by describing the worst people developer they can imagine;
then the best.)  This session focuses on attitude and behaviour,
rather than on role.
How good a mentor are you?

What makes a good protege?     10 mins
Parallel session, looking at the characteristics of a protege.

12:30pm
Lunch

1:15pm
The roles of a mentor     60 mins

A close look at what mentors do.
Plenum exercise to evolve a list of roles, to which
facilitator(s) will add as necessary.
In groups of three or four, participants will develop examples
from their own experience or imagination, as to how these roles
should be fulfilled and the situations, in which they might
apply.  Using these or supplied situations (eg from the Kit),
each group will defend its particular approach to solving the
issue.

The four key roles of coaching, counselling, networking and
facilitating will be drawn out in particular detail.
```

Example 2 continued

```
The mentoring contract   40 minutes
Plenum discussion of the nature of a contract:
- administrative elements
- learning goals

Exercise: in pairs, design the kind of contract they would wish
to apply.  (Each puts self on an alternating basis into the
protege's shoes.)

What could go wrong?     30 mins
General plenum discussion


An agenda for the first meeting    30 mins
In pairs, decide on what they want to discuss and how they will
arrange the meeting to get the relationship off to a good start

Wrap up and review  15 mins
Final questions, answers and comments
Ends circa 6pm
```

Example 3 **A programme for all parties engaged in organization-wide mentoring: Henley Distance Learning**

Henley Distance Learning have established an excellent distance learning kit which is available from Henley Distance Learning. Of all the kits examined, *The mentoring kit* written by David Clutterbuck (1992) is the most comprehensive guide currently available for would-be mentors, protégés and organizations. Developed as a 'trainer/line manager' module within the Henley portfolio of management development materials, it is presented in workbook form for completion by those preparing to mentor. Main sections deal with:

- Why do we need mentors?
- What is a mentor?
- The key roles of mentoring
- Managing the mentoring relationship
- Mentoring pitfalls

The guide prompts thought about the mentor relationship and asks questions throughout. Answers to these questions are provided. Case studies are provided to illustrate the sections, providing examples of criteria for a good mentor; reasons why mentoring does not work; benefits to all involved; an audit process and the different elements which various schemes incorporate.

The workbook is supplemented by specific documents which would be completed by the mentor and protégé, including a questionnaire designed to examine the suitability of the person for the role of a mentor; agenda for the first meeting; an outline contract; a SWOT analysis form; action planning form; setting development tasks outline; a mentoring review and assessment form; a protégé briefing sheet and a protégé preparation form.

Example 4 **Training programmes for librarians: The Burrington Partnership:**

This workshop was designed for The Library Association's Continuing Education Department by the Burrington Partnership. It was aimed at those individuals who wished to develop mentoring skills for adaptation and use in libraries. The following description offers a guide to the only library-specific training course currently available.

On being a mentor
Workshop Tutor: Dr Gill Burrington
Programme

Session 1 The purpose and benefits of mentoring
The broad purposes of mentoring are presented as being psychosocial and economic. Areas of mentoring to be addressed are illustrated: these include skill development, knowledge development and behaviour modification.

The benefits to the individual being mentored, the organization, the profession and the mentor are all given.

Session 2 Formal and informal mentoring schemes
This session evaluates the advantages and disadvantages of each of the two schemes.

Session 3 Setting up a mentoring scheme
The considerations for the establishment of a mentoring scheme are provided, starting with the purpose and scope of the scheme, the selection of the mentor and the choice of mentor for a protégé. Some guidance about the allocation of time and commitment are provided.

Session 4 Group work
The group is requested to list the knowledge which a mentor will need.

Session 5 Skills mentors need
The core skills are listed as communication, encouraging and confidence building, enthusing, evaluating, informing/coaching/teaching, listening, observing, questioning, confronting and criticising.

Session 6 Practising the skills of a mentor
A workshop designed to confirm the understanding of the previous session.

Session 7 The way forward
This session requires participants to actively but critically evaluate their strengths and approach to mentoring. This needs to be undertaken before successful mentoring, whether formal or informal is undertaken.

END

Course held 30 September 1993 and 8 February 1994
© The Burrington Partnership 1993

Example 5 | **Open learning materials for library staff: NTG & SCET**

One of a series of learning packages tailor-made for librarians and information managers and designed for staff responsible for financial or other resources.

Northern Training Group (NTG) and Scottish Council for Education Technology (SCET), *Financial management for librarians*, ISBN 1 898725 00 4.

Price: £55 per pack plus postage. Available from: Information North, Quaker Meeting House, 1 Archbold Terrace, Newcastle upon Tyne, NE2 1DB. Tel: 091 281 8887

Example 6 | **Mentoring to improve performance: ITD Training Limited**

This ITD Training Limited course is for those committed to accelerating the learning and development of those less experienced. Those gaining benefit from this course will include human resource specialists, senior managers and those involved with professional institutions' activities.

Objectives
This course will enable mentoring to be implemented effectively in an organization, and includes:

- Developing an effective strategy to implement mentoring
- Selecting and training mentors
- Implementing appropriate supporting documentation
- Selling the concept to senior management
- Giving mentors effective tools to enable them to accelerate the development of others

Content
- What is mentoring?
- The link with coaching and counselling
- Effective models which mentors can use
- Factors in the choice of mentors
- Establishing the right relationship
- Supporting the relationship with appropriate documentation including logbooks and personal development plans
- Implementing a strategy for mentoring in your organization

Outcomes
- A plan for implementing a mentoring culture
- Specifications for identifying probable mentors
- Checklists for developing the right environment
- An awareness of mentoring skills
- Examples of appropriate support documentation

The ITD also hold national and international mentoring events aiming to bring together academics and consultants, human resource professionals and those who are in mentoring relationships, to share the latest thinking and research in mentoring.

Such events provide networking opportunities as well as workshops and syndicates for specific skills development, or issues of importance when considering the implementation of mentoring.

| Example 7 | **Professional development for women: Women into Information Technology** |

The α, β, γ of Mentoring is a professional development workshop designed specifically for women by the Women into Information Technology Foundation Limited (WIT), which recognizes the increasing use of mentoring as an effective form of professional training and development.

Contributors and their presentations at WIT mentoring day events have included:-

- Ellen Neighbour, Operations Director WIT
  The IT manager of the 90's - the mentoring programme in perspective
- Viki Holton, Senior Researcher, Ashridge Management Group
  Mentoring - an overview, national and international programmes
- Jenny Sweeney, Senior consultant, The Industrial Society
  Mastering mentoring - a practical guide
- Victoria Hillier, Equal Opportunities Manager, BT
  Mentoring and networking - application in BT
- Maureen Atkinson, Head of Professional Women's Development Network, Staffordshire University
  The Staffordshire University mentoring project
- Phil Dickinson, Learning Consultant, ICL Staff Learning
  The ICL self-development programme - mentoring scheme
- Lesley Berry, Management Consultant, Henley Distance Learning Ltd.
  The Henley mentoring kit

Example 8 **Mentoring for senior managers: Roffey Park Management Institute**

The following is an example of a training workshop for Senior Managers.

Outline of tailored workshop on mentoring

9.00 — Outline and discussion of desired outcomes for this workshop day
Purposes and goals in mentoring in this organisation
Organisational points (question and answer)

10.00 — Checklist of possible mentoring roles
Overview of "Four Diamonds" model
Key behaviours, mind-sets, assumptions that help
and hinder in the mentoring process

10.30 — Skills practice, role-play on mini-scenarios
(using typical moments in a mentoring situation in
the context of this organisation)

11.00 — Coffee

11.15 — Listening, attending and hearing
Barriers to listening
(Discussion and input)

11.30 — Skills practice in listening, reflecting clarifying and
summarising

12.00 — Establishing ground-rules and boundaries
Phases in the mentoring relationship
Review: how are we doing?
(Discussion)

12.30 — Lunch

1.30 — Establishing rapport
Non-verbal communication and body language
(Discussion, input and role-play)

2.30 — Understanding another person's perspective
(structured activity)

3.00 — Review of learning. Practice with longer scenario

4.30 — Planning and recording of mentoring work

5.00 — Review and close

(Inputs, exercises and discussions will be supported by printed material
which as a set form a useful handbook for mentors and others involved
in 1:1 developmental situations)

© Roffey Park Management Institute 1994

Appendix D
Glossary of terms used within the text

Benchmark A specific point, recognized by those involved, in any development or initiative.

Dyad A group comprising two people, in this case the mentor and the protégé.

Learning organization An organization which is concerned with growing and expanding through development, not just the development of the employees but of the organization itself. This is not a simple response to change, but is a positive seeking out and testing of ideas.

Life mentor A mentor who has an interest in the protégé's life as well as career. Life mentors may also advise on a protégé's career.

Major mentor A mentor who establishes all three of the following components in the mentoring relationship with a protégé: attraction, action and affect.

Mentee An alternative term for protégé (see below).

Mentor In current usage, a trusted person who provides advice and guidance to a younger, or less experienced, individual. Some definitions distinguish between professional development and personal development.

Mentoring system A strategy adopted by organizations who wish to encourage older, or more experienced employees, to assist in the development of new members of staff. The system is generally a human resource development, but may have origins in any part of the organization. The best systems are introduced with full commitment from senior managers.

Mind set The existence of a particular attitude which is resistant to change and modification. This can come about as a result of cultural or organizational conditioning.

Minor mentor A mentor who fulfils less than three of the components necessary to be a major mentor (see above).

Organizational culture The creation of a specific set of values and behaviours within an organization. These will influence employees, leading them towards particular behavioural patterns in keeping with the organization's ethos.

Partial mentor One of several advisors or mentors which a person may establish over the course of their lives or careers. These mentors are usually informal mentors, but may offer guidance on a protégé's career.

Primary mentor A term used by some authors to distinguish mentors who establish an emotional bond with a protégé from those for whom career or professional mentoring is the only contract.

Protégé The protégé is the person who is receiving the wisdom and experience passed on to them by a guide or adviser in either formal or informal mentoring.

Quasi mentor According to some writers, a mentor who only has a career-development mentoring brief.

Secondary mentor A mentor established by a protégé, usually in an informal way, to assist with a specific area of the protégé's life. Protégés can establish a number of secondary mentors throughout their lives. (See also partial mentors.)

Succession planning In order to ensure that there are suitable candidates for promotion within a company, some organizations will engage in planning the future of certain employees who are seen to fit the criteria necessary for particular senior roles at some later stage in their careers. This 'grooming' will certainly include mentoring from an existing senior manager, or similarly placed person.

Index

Other Library Training Guides available

Training needs analysis
Michael Williamson
1-85604-077-1

Induction
Julie Parry
1-85604-078-X

Evaluation
Steve Phillips
1-85604-079-8

Training and development for women
Beryl Morris
1-85604-080-1

Interpersonal skills
Philippa Levy
1-85604-081-X

Management of training and staff development
June Whetherly
1-85604-104-2

Recruitment
Julie Parry
1-85604-106-9
Forthcoming

*Supporting adult learners: training for open learning in library
and information work*
Tony Bamber et al
1-85604-125-5
Forthcoming